8/17

The
ALLERGY-FREE
BABY &
TODDLER
COOKBOOK

The
ALLERGY-FREE
BABY &
TODDLER
COOKBOOK

Fiona Heggie & Ellie Lux

First published in Great Britain in 2016
by Orion Publishing Group Ltd
Carmelite House, 50 Victoria Embankment
London EC4Y 0DZ
An Hachette UK Company

10 9 8 7 6 5 4 3 2 1

Text © Fiona Heggie and Ellie Lux 2016
Design and layout © Orion Publishing Group Ltd 2016

A CIP catalogue record for this book
is available from the British Library.

ISBN: 978-0-2976-0836-3

Photography: Andrew Burton
Art direction: Abi Hartshorne
Design: Clare Sivell
Props: Tamzin Ferdinando
Home economist: Georgie Besterman

Printed and bound in China

The Orion Publishing Group's policy is to use papers that
are natural, renewable and recyclable products and made
from wood grown in sustainable forests. The logging and
manufacturing processes are expected to conform to the
environmental regulations of the country of origin.

www.orionbooks.co.uk

For more delicious recipes, features, videos and
exclusives from Orion's cookery writers, and to
sign up for our 'Recipe of the Week' email visit
bybookorbycook.co.uk

Follow us
 @bybookorbycook    @bybookorbycook

Find us
 facebook.com/bybookorbycook

CONTENTS

Introduction

Introducing your baby to real food for the first time is one of the many great joys of parenthood. It is a time when your child starts using yet another of their senses to experience the world around them. And, as with all major developmental landmarks, you and your child will need to learn on the job, figuring out what works and what doesn't as you go.

That process is somewhat complicated if your child is diagnosed with a food allergy. The good news is, as with most other aspects of parenting, there are very few things that you are likely to come across that someone else hasn't already experienced.

When it comes to weaning children with food allergies, we are two mums who have been there, done that and got the baby food-spattered T-shirts. We would like to offer some practical advice on weaning children with food allergies and to share some of our experience.

There are more than 100 recipes in this book that cover the whole weaning process and beyond. They are all free from 14 common allergens. We hope they will help make your life easier and provide your baby with enjoyable first tastes that will set them up for a lifetime of healthy eating. The book is also packed with handy tips and advice that will help with the day-to-day practicalities of managing food allergies.

We recognise that most babies are not allergic to all 14 allergens and indeed some of them such as sulphites, celery and mustard very rarely cause reactions in children. Dairy, eggs, soya, nuts and sesame are the most common food allergies in children but even so it is unusual for a baby or child to be allergic to all of them. So, most of the recipes contain suggestions for how you can add things back in, like cheese for example, if your child isn't allergic to dairy, or you can swap chicken for fish. A food allergy, or multiple allergies, will restrict your baby's diet already; there's no point in restricting it further than necessary.

If you are reading this it will probably be because your baby has been diagnosed with a food allergy, multiple food allergies or maybe a food intolerance. Multiple food allergies are becoming increasingly common and it can sometimes take a while for further allergies to become apparent even after the first has been diagnosed. If your baby hasn't been diagnosed but you suspect he or she may have an allergy or intolerance, we urge you to see your GP in order to be referred to a specialist.

If you are breastfeeding you may need to avoid the foods to which your baby is allergic. For those that this applies to, many recipes in this book make delicious meals for adults – perhaps with a little added seasoning – to save you cooking twice. However an elimination diet should not be embarked on without discussing this with a doctor or dietitian to ensure that your diet is not deficient in nutrients.

Some babies take to weaning very naturally while others are a little more reluctant, but they all get there in the end. The process is identical for those with or without allergies – you're simply omitting some ingredients. Even if your child has

an allergy, there's still a whole world of food out there for them to try. There's no reason babies with a food allergy shouldn't enjoy their food just as much as other babies.

We've given some practical advice on what to look out for on food labels, avoiding food contamination at home and what to do as and when your baby goes to play groups and day care. Throughout the book we've also shared our personal experience of managing our own children's allergies and making sure they don't miss out.

MEDICAL ADVICE

Throughout the book we often suggest following your doctor's advice. This book is not the place to give specific detailed information relating to things like how to introduce potential allergens into your child's diet. Every child's set of circumstances is different; your child's doctor will take into account a host of factors such as family history, test results, related conditions such as eczema and respiratory complications as well as whether your baby's allergy is immediate (also called IgE-mediated) or delayed (also called non-IgE-mediated) – see page 12 for more information. Your child's doctor will use their training, experience and expertise to assess all this information to give a diagnosis, and will also be able to give detailed guidance on diet. Only a qualified doctor specialising in allergy and immunology can do this. Our book is based on our experience as parents, and is limited to practical advice and delicious recipes.

OUR STORIES

Isabelle, Ellie's elder daughter, has immediate food allergy to dairy, egg, peanut and sesame. She had very bad eczema as a baby that required the use of nightly bandages and several creams until she was 18 months old. Looking back, we now know that the eczema was a reaction to the proteins in cow's milk that were being passed on to her through breast milk.

We conclusively discovered Isabelle was allergic to dairy when she tried a piece of cheese in the early days of weaning: within moments of sucking on her first chunk of Cheddar, she came out in hives across her whole body and her eyes puffed up and closed. The GP referred Isabelle to a specialist and she subsequently tested positive for allergies to egg and peanuts too. It took a bit longer for her allergy to sesame to be diagnosed, as tests initially came back negative. It was only when she reacted to hummus that we knew this was a problem food for her as well.

To complete the picture she is also allergic to house dust mites and dogs, and suffers from hay fever. She has asthma, which has resulted in several hospital stays – the first time when she was eight months old. Isabelle's asthma, among other factors, makes it likely she will have an anaphylactic reaction if exposed to foods she's allergic to, so she carries adrenaline auto-injectors as well as her inhalers and antihistamine in a little backpack wherever she goes.

Casper, Fiona's son, has a combination of immediate food allergy like Isabelle to egg and peanuts. He also has non-immediate food allergy, the diagnosis of which was not so straightforward. From birth he had various gastrointestinal problems and suffered terribly with painful reflux. Some of his symptoms were eventually attributed to delayed allergy to gluten. Casper had to endure numerous hospital tests and it took months of restrictive elimination diets to find the cause.

His allergies have persisted, and even now some of his other gastrointestinal problems can be alleviated by eliminating dairy and soya from his diet. It has been a continual struggle to keep his weight up and to make sure that he is getting a high-energy diet.

So, if you're going through something similar, we know how daunting it can be. We remember it being particularly tough in the early days. Eliminating multiple allergens from our children's diets is something we have had to learn to deal with. It is our hope that we can share some tips and recipes to help make your life easier if you are facing the same challenges.

It is, at this point, worth highlighting the positives. Yes, the early days will prove to be a steep learning curve. But we have found that your child's food allergy doesn't have to dominate your life. Don't let anyone tell you food allergies are not serious; they are and can have life-threatening consequences. Nevertheless, we have found that, if you take sensible precautions, there is no reason why your children can't fully participate in all that life has to offer.

We certainly don't feel our children miss out on anything or that they are defined by their food allergies. That was true when they were babies and it is true now that they're older: they join in virtually all the same activities as their peers at nursery and school. They go to birthday parties, on play dates and on school trips; they eat out at restaurants like everyone else. In fact, it is incredible how quickly it becomes perfectly normal to check labels, quiz staff in restaurants and communicate with school and nursery staff.

Fiona has always been passionate about food and, before her children were born, trained at Leith's School of Food and Wine and ran a successful London-based catering business. When our babies were diagnosed with food allergies we both went about developing nutritious recipes suitable for their set of allergies, and later enjoyed experimenting and creating delicious meals that the whole family could enjoy together – and we'd now like to share some of those recipes with you.

OUR PHILOSOPHY

- Food allergy needn't mean your baby can't eat a broad range of tasty food.
- Food allergy doesn't have to define your baby or dominate your life.
- Any parent can make our simple, allergy-friendly recipes.
- Having a food allergy doesn't mean your baby has to miss out on treats.
- We believe in using ordinary, fresh, easy-to-obtain ingredients.
- Weaning should be just as fun for a baby with a food allergy as one without.
- The more children are exposed to a wide variety of ingredients, flavours and textures, the more likely they are to be adventurous eaters as they grow up.

ORGANIC FOOD

We think it makes sense to use fruit and vegetables that have been treated with as few chemicals as possible. In the case of organic meat, there are also tight restrictions on the use of antibiotics and other medicines. Organically reared animals tend to be treated better too, which we believe is important. While we know it is more expensive, we believe it's worth buying organic if you can.

SUSTAINABLE FISH

If your child is not allergic to fish, we would urge you to buy it from sustainable sources. This means avoiding fish varieties that are overfished, from poorly managed fisheries or caught using methods that can harm other marine life. We hope that by buying fish responsibly we'll help ensure that there is a wide variety of different fish for our children to choose from when they grow up.

ENDORSED BY MEDICAL EXPERTS

This book is based on our personal experience as two mums who manage food allergy on a daily basis. However *The Allergy-Free Baby & Toddler Cookbook* has also been reviewed and endorsed by two medical experts specialising in food allergy: Dr Helen Cox and Dr Rosan Meyer.

Dr Cox is a paediatric allergy and immunology consultant, lecturing all over the world and based at Imperial College NHS Trust. She has reviewed this book, ensuring that all the content is sound and reliable, and she has written a very useful chapter answering many questions parents with newly diagnosed babies often ask. She gives an excellent overview of food allergy and cuts through its complexity.

Dr Meyer, who is a paediatric allergy dietitian, has reviewed this book and all the recipes from a nutritional perspective, so you can be certain that the recipes are balanced, nutritious and free from major allergens.

Both have a wealth of practical experience, having seen hundreds of children with multiple food allergies in their clinics. We are extremely grateful to them for their support and their valuable contribution to this book.

We'd very much like to thank nutritional therapist Jane Thatcher-Browne who has also reviewed this book and provided invaluable input. She trained at the renowned Institute of Optimum Nutrition, following which she set up her own clinical practice and advised at Sprint Physiotherapy Clinic in London.

In reviewing this book, she has given general nutritional advice, as well as making sure all the recipes are nutritious and form part of a healthy, balanced diet.

This book cannot in any way replace the need for your baby to be seen by an expert in allergy, so please do not use this book unless your child has been assessed by a specialist. It is intended as a practical guide and as a recipe book for those babies and toddlers who have been diagnosed as having a food allergy or intolerance by a doctor.

FOOD ALLERGY
Explained by Dr Helen Cox

WHAT ARE FOOD ALLERGIES AND WHEN DO THEY OCCUR?

The majority of food allergies present within the first two years of life as infants are introduced to new milk formulas and foods. The reactions can occur at any stage with some babies reacting within the first few weeks of life. Food allergic reactions occur when the body recognises a food protein as being 'foreign'. This generates a strong immune response aimed at rejecting that food protein, leading to a range of symptoms affecting different parts of the body. Broadly speaking these immune-mediated reactions can be divided into immediate and delayed reactions.

IMMEDIATE REACTIONS occur within minutes to two hours of eating the food. They can be provoked by minute quantities of food protein which binds to allergen specific IgE receptors in the body leading to the release of histamine and other inflammatory mediators. These reactions occur each and every time the food is given. Allergy tests (skin prick tests and IgE blood tests) are usually positive. The reactions can trigger a range of responses involving the skin, gut, respiratory and cardiovascular systems. Immediate redness and itching of the skin followed by the development of hives (urticaria) occur commonly. This can be accompanied by swelling of the lips, eyes, face hands and feet (angioedema). Vomiting also occurs frequently as the body attempts to rid itself of the allergen. Skin reactions usually resolve rapidly after withdrawal of the food allergen and respond well to treatment with antihistamine.

More severe reactions involve either the respiratory or cardiovascular systems. This may lead to the development of breathing difficulties with a persistent cough, wheeze, noisy breathing or voice change due to swelling of the airway. Alternatively, reactions may lead to a drop in blood pressure resulting in extreme pallor, floppiness, drowsiness or even collapse. These severe reactions are called 'anaphylaxis' and require immediate medical attention with the administration of injectable adrenaline.

DELAYED REACTIONS to foods are more insidious in onset and therefore more difficult to diagnose. The reactions typically occur within one to three days of eating the food leading to a range of symptoms affecting either the skin or gut. They usually require larger amounts of allergen to provoke a reaction. Allergy tests are usually negative. Typical symptoms can include one or more of the following: eczema, vomiting, reflux, colic, abdominal pain, constipation, diarrhoea, blood or mucous in the stools or faltering growth. Occasionally the vomiting can occur within minutes of eating and be severe and protracted leading to dehydration and collapse needing urgent medical attention. The term food protein-enterocolitis (FPIES) has been used to describe these reactions, which may be accompanied by bloody stools.

As many of these symptoms can occur in non-allergic infants it is often the co-association of features that makes the diagnosis more likely. Faltering growth is a worrying sign of possible malabsorption and requires urgent review. It is worth pointing out, however, that many babies with delayed food allergy have normal growth parameters.

WHICH FOODS CAUSE REACTIONS?

Any one of the 14 foods listed by the EU are capable of causing an immediate reaction. In the first two years of life the main culprits are cow's milk, eggs and nuts, which account for three-quarters of immediate reactions, followed by sesame, wheat, fish, soya, kiwi and, rarely, shellfish. Allergy to pulses (lentils, chickpeas, peas) occurs more frequently in Asian and vegan populations reflecting their higher consumption of these foods. Sulphites very rarely cause adverse reactions in infants.

The list of foods causing delayed reactions is shorter with four main food proteins causing most reactions. Cow's milk causes the majority of delayed reactions followed by soya, gluten (wheat, barley, rye, oats) and lastly eggs. Approximately half of all infants with delayed reactions to cow's milk also react to soya with similar symptoms.

Certain foods such as tomatoes and berries are high in natural histamines leading to mild rashes around the mouth post ingestion. Acidic foods such as pineapples and oranges can also aggravate the skin of a baby with eczema. These foods cause irritation as opposed to allergic reactions.

WHAT TO DO IF YOU SUSPECT YOUR CHILD IS FOOD ALLERGIC?

It is best to seek medical help early if you suspect that your child is food allergic. This not only ensures that an accurate diagnosis is made but also allows your child to progress with their weaning diet in a safe manner while ensuring that their diet is as nutritious and varied as possible. This usually requires the support of a children's allergy doctor and dietitian. Although these recipes are free from 14 allergens, it would be foolish to avoid allergens if this was not necessary, so add in the appropiate suggested optional extras.

As allergists, once food allergy is diagnosed we would actively promote the early introduction and inclusion of a diverse range of 'permitted foods' while excluding a baby's known allergens. In support of this approach a recent study has found that including peanuts early into the diet of infants with eczema and egg allergy, significantly reduced the risk of having a peanut allergy at five years. In high risk infants with eczema and/or other food allergies, allergy testing prior to introduction is recommended.

WHEN TO ALLERGY TEST?

Testing food allergens can be carried out in infants from the age of three to four months and to inhalant allergens from the age of 12 months. Both skin prick tests and blood specific IgE tests are able to detect the presence of allergen specific IgE antibodies and this does not rely upon a prior history of food ingestion. The tests are very useful to diagnose or exclude immediate food allergy. They are also able to assess a child's risk of reacting to a food not yet introduced. They are particularly useful in infants with moderate to severe eczema where the tests can help guide decisions regarding dietary elimination and inclusions. They do however require a skilled practitioner to interpret the tests in the light of the clinical history, as the tests are fraught with difficulty with both false positive and false negative reactions occurring. Food challenge tests are often needed where the diagnosis is still uncertain based on borderline test results.

There are no validated tests to diagnose delayed food allergy. Food Intolerance tests measuring IgE antibodies and other alternative tests have no role in the diagnosis of either immediate or delayed food allergy. The diagnosis of delayed allergy is made based on pattern recognition of symptoms followed by the implementation of a trial period of dietary elimination followed by challenge tests.

In formula-fed infants with suspected cow's milk allergy, a prescribed hypo-allergenic milk formula may be offered for a trial period. In breastfed infants, a trial period of removing cow's milk and soya from the maternal diet for four weeks may be suggested. Dietetic support and maternal calcium supplementation during such dietary implementation is important. Formula milks that are **unsuitable** for treating cow's milk allergy in young infants include goat's milk, lactose-free milk and soya milk in addition to most anti-reflux formulas which are based on cow's milk protein.

WHICH INFANTS ARE AT HIGHER RISK OF BEING FOOD ALLERGIC?

Having one or both parents with either asthma, hayfever or eczema or a sibling with food allergy will increase an infant's risk of food allergy. Being allergic to one food will also increase an infant's chance of reacting to other foods, with two-thirds of those children being allergic to more than one food. Another high risk group are infants who develop persistent eczema within the first few months of life despite treatment with topical steroids and emollients. The risk rises with increasing eczema severity ranging between 30–60 per cent. These infants are also at greater risk of developing either asthma or hayfever in a progression known as 'the atopic march'.

Ideally these infants should be referred early for an allergy assessment and testing to inform on the weaning diet. If your baby is deemed to be high risk and is still waiting to be seen by a doctor, then it would be advisable to introduce foods of low allergenic potential first. When introducing foods that are capable of causing an allergic reaction, this needs to be done cautiously starting with a tiny amount of food touched to the inside of the lip, followed by small amounts of the food given at least an hour apart, in increasing incremental amounts over three days.

I am often struck by how varied and healthy the diets are of children with food allergy who I see in clinic. Dietary restrictions inevitably mean less junk food and more home cooking using fresh ingredients. This recipe book is brimming with creative ideas and delicious recipes to wean and feed your allergic baby.

1

Your Baby's Nutrition

KEY INFORMATION ABOUT 14 FOOD ALLERGENS

1 Dairy
2 Eggs
3 Peanuts
4 Tree nuts
5 Soya
6 Wheat and gluten-containing grains
7 Sesame
8 Fish
9 Molluscs
10 Crustaceans
11 Celery
12 Mustard
13 Lupin
14 Sulphites

The allergens excluded from our recipes are regarded by the EU as major allergens. EU legislation stipulates that these allergens must be highlighted on ingredient lists on manufactured food, usually in bold, but sometimes italics or underlined. In restaurants, delis and bakeries, they must be highlighted either on the menu or blackboard or verbally via a waiter or server. This makes life easier for those with food allergy to identify allergens, especially those that aren't immediately obvious.

The overviews of the allergens in the chart overleaf give advice on foods to avoid and foods in which you might not expect to find allergens. The lists aren't exhaustive but aim to give you an idea of the sorts of foods that might contain hidden allergens. It's always important to check labels or ask in restaurants every time you eat, as ingredients and processes can change surprisingly regularly. Although many of the items on these lists are things your baby can't or shouldn't eat until they are older, we've included them in case you are a breastfeeding mother who needs to avoid allergens and also so you have them in mind as your child grows up. A vegan symbol means that there are no animal products contained in the food, including dairy, fish, shellfish or eggs, but always check the label carefully for other allergens.

'MAY CONTAIN' STATEMENTS

Be aware that many labels may include voluntary warnings to indicate whether a food that doesn't actually contain an allergen was prepared or packaged in an environment containing allergens.

The chances of contamination could be great or small, and you need to discuss with your baby's doctor or dietitian whether or not your baby should have these foods. These statements are entirely voluntary and there is no legal requirement for a manufacturer to include one. It is therefore worth noting that just because a product doesn't carry this warning, doesn't necessarily make it a safer bet than a product that does.

OVERVIEW OF 14 EU ALLERGENS

ALLERGEN	FOODS TO AVOID	FOODS TO BE WARY OF Usually or sometimes contain the allergen
DAIRY	Cow's milk, cream, butter, cheese, yoghurt, ice cream, other animal milk (as the proteins that cause allergic reactions are very similar) and derivatives	Margarines (including sunflower and olive oil-based varieties), biscuits and cakes, chocolate, fudge, toffee, anything in batter or made from batter such as pancakes, Yorkshire puddings and tempura, sausages, breaded/crumbed chicken, fish fingers, soups and sauces such as béchamel, pesto, breakfast cereals, lactose-free foods and drinks (unless also dairy-free)
EGGS	Egg in all forms (poached, baked, fried, scrambled, boiled, omelettes)	Cakes, pastry, biscuits, meringues, puddings, custards, mousses, royal icing, marzipan, sauces, condiments (such as tartare, horseradish, Béarnaise, hollandaise and mayonnaise), pasta and noodles, ice cream, sorbets, sausages, burgers (both veggie and meat), meatballs, fish fingers, breaded/crumbed chicken, anything in batter or made from batter such as pancakes, Yorkshire puddings and tempura, stock cubes, gravy, marshmallows, chocolate bars, brioche, sweet buns, gluten-free bread, glazed rolls, microprotein meat substitutes
PEANUTS AND TREE NUTS	Nuts themselves, praline, satay, nut oils, peanut butter, other nut butters	Marzipan, nougat, chocolate bars, chocolate brownies, sauces, (such as pesto and korma), nut-based cakes and biscuits (such as Christmas cake), breakfast cereal, cereal bars, veggie burgers, popcorn
SOYA	Soya beans, soya milk, 'yoghurts' and puddings, tofu, meat alternatives, miso, soya and tamari sauces, unrefined soya oil, soya-based meat substitutes, edamame beans	Breakfast cereals, bread, cakes, pizza bases, biscuits tinned soup, crackers, crisps, ready-made desserts, ice cream, chocolate, margarine, processed beef burgers, meat pies, minced beef, sausages and hot-dogs, pancake and waffle mixes, pasta, ready meals, sauces including Worcester sauce, sweet and sour sauce, Teriyaki sauce, mayonnaise and salad cream, stock cubes and gravy
GLUTEN	Wheat, barley, rye, oats (due to cross contamination), spelt, bulgur wheat, kamut, all baked goods containing gluten-containing flour such as bread, cakes, biscuits, pastry, pizza bases etc, porridge, pasta, cous cous	Breakfast cereals, cereal bars, sausages, burgers, meatballs, fish fingers, breaded chicken, anything in batter or made from batter such as pancakes, Yorkshire puddings and tempura, white sauces like béchamel or cheese sauces with a roux (flour, butter, milk) base and other sauces, soya sauce, potato products like chips, crisps and roast potatoes (sometimes lightly coated in flour to make them crispy), flavoured crisps, soups, gravy and stock cubes

ALLERGEN	FOODS TO AVOID	FOODS TO BE WARY OF Usually or sometimes contain the allergen
SESAME	Sesame seeds, tahini paste (used in hummus), sesame oil	Dips, especially Greek and Middle Eastern ones like aubergine dips and hummus, sausages, burgers, veggie burgers, margarines and spreads, chocolate bars and flapjacks, baked goods such as bread, buns, bagels, biscuits and breadsticks, cereal bars, salad dressings and chutney, stir-fry sauces and curry sauces, garnishes on salads and vegetables
FISH	Flaky fish such as cod and haddock, meaty fish such as tuna and swordfish, oily fish such as trout and salmon, flat fish such as sole and plaice, round fish such as bream and mullet, fish fingers, oriental fish sauce, fish stock, fish soup, fish pie	Shellfish soup such as lobster bisque, shellfish platters, Worcester sauce (anchovy is often found in mince dishes such as shepherd's/cottage pie and bolognese that uses Worcester sauce), Caesar salad dressing (anchovies), foods containing fish sauce such as stir-fries, Thai food, Vietnamese curries and Chinese cuisine, marshmallows and nougat (can contain fish gelatin)
MOLLUSCS AND CRUSTACEANS	**Molluscs:** Gastropods such as periwinkles, and whelks, Bivalves such as mussels, scallops, clams and oysters, cephalapods such as octopus, squid and cuttlefish. **Crustaceans** such as prawns, lobsters, crabs, crayfish, shrimps, langoustines	Fish stock, fish soup such as bouillabaisse, sauces such as bisque, oriental fish sauce, marinara sauce, pasta sauces (even tomato-based sauces can contain shellfish), Indian and Thai curry pastes, sushi (even if it doesn't obviously contain shellfish, be aware that cross-contamination could have occurred), dietary supplements like fish oil sometimes contain shellfish
CELERY	Celery in all its forms, celeriac	Stock cubes, bouillon and gravy, soups, sauces, stews and casseroles, salads, tomato juice, spice mixes, crisps, Marmite
MUSTARD	Jars of mustard, mustard seeds, mustard flowers, mustard leaves	Sauces such as barbecue sauce, béchamel, hollandaise, mayonnaise and salad cream, glazed or marinated meat, salad dressings, processed meats such as sausages, Indian curries, bread or buns (sometimes contain mustard seeds)
LUPIN	Lupin seeds, lupin beans; lupin flour, which can be found in baked goods such as bread and pastry	Baked goods including bread, pastry, pancakes, waffles, crumbed foods, pasta (including gluten-free varieties), flour (including gluten-free varieties), burgers and sausages
SULPHITES	It is possible to find sulphite-free versions of most products, but they can be hard to source	Dried fruit such as apricots, mangoes, peaches, raisins, sultanas and currants, pickled foods such as beetroot and onions, processed and cured meats and fish such as ham and bacon, frozen shellfish, wine and beer, some condiments such as vinegar

DAIRY

Dairy allergy is very common among babies, but the good news is that the majority of children outgrow their allergy in childhood – often quite quickly. Milk and dairy products make up a whole food group that is an essential part of everyone's diet, so it can be particularly daunting if this is an allergen you need to cut out. It contains protein and also key nutrients – most notably calcium (crucial for strong bones and teeth) – that are important in all diets but especially so in those of babies and children. If you are still breastfeeding, a dietitian will advise whether you should cut dairy out of your own diet, and what foods and supplements (such as calcium and vitamin D) you'll need to take to ensure you are getting sufficient nutrients for you and your baby. Your baby's dietitian can also advise on and prescribe a hypoallergenic formula that contains key nutrients your baby would otherwise get from a dairy-based formula. As your baby gets older, your dietitian will be able to offer advice on other foods your baby should have to ensure they are getting enough calcium, protein and other nutrients from alternative sources, and they can also advise on supplements.

After the age of one some babies will be ready to move on to an alternative milk to breast milk or hypoallergenic formula. This will very much depend on individual circumstances based on the child's current diet, feeding behaviour and growth. Others will be advised to continue with their hypoallergenic formula in order to meet all of their nutritional requirements. With the exception of soya milk, all of the fortified non-formula milk alternatives (rice, oat, almond, coconut), while having similar amounts of calcium to cow's milk

(120mg per 100ml), have far lower levels of protein and fat. They are therefore not suitable for a baby under 12 months old or for infants over the age of one with suboptimal growth or those on highly restricted diets.

We offer some suggestions for calcium-rich foods that you may like to consider adding to your child's diet as an *extra* source of calcium. However, it is important to note that this must be in addition to a hypoallergenic formula or breast milk when your baby is still having these, and in addition to your dietitian's recommended alternative milk for your toddler or older child. Babies and toddlers rely mainly on breast milk or formula for their daily calcium intake and calcium from vegetable sources is much harder for the body to absorb so these need to be seen as supplementary sources of calcium to your child's diet. We try to include many of the foods listed on the page opposite in Isabelle and Casper's diets whenever we can, so we have included some of them in our recipes, and we also make suggestions at the bottom of recipes for adding some of the allergens from the second list if your child is not allergic to them.

On food labels dairy will usually be highlighted on the ingredients list as **milk**, although it is worth noting that some products may list butter, yoghurt or cream instead, as these are considered to be clearly derived from milk.

Other animal milks such as sheep's, goat's, buffalo's or camel's milk are not suitable for those with dairy allergy, as the proteins that cause allergic reactions are very similar in all animal milks. Similarly, lactose-free milks are not suitable for dairy allergy sufferers (see box opposite).

CALCIUM BOOSTS

- Seaweed, dried nori
- Fresh figs
- Spinach
- Watercress
- Curly kale
- Dried pineapple
- Purple sprouting broccoli
- Sunflower seeds
- Red kidney beans
- Broccoli, steamed
- Okra

If your child is not allergic, you can also add:

- Tahini (sesame paste found in hummus)
- Sesame seeds
- Tinned sardines (mashed)
- Tofu
- Tinned salmon (mashed)
- Almonds, hazelnuts, walnuts (crushed) or nut butters
- Tinned mackerel (mashed)
- Soya puddings
- Soya milk

ALLERGIC TO DAIRY OR LACTOSE INTOLERANT – WHAT'S THE DIFFERENCE?

The immune systems of those allergic to dairy react to the proteins in the milk, which their bodies mistakenly interpret as harmful. Lactose intolerance is related to the carbohydrate in cow's milk – lactose – and occurs due to a deficiency in the enzyme lactase which is needed to process lactose. There are two types of lactose intolerance: primary and secondary. With primary lactose intolerance a reduction in the enzyme lactase occurs over time. Primary lactose intolerance is more common in African and Asian populations. Typically those with primary lactose intolerance cannot tolerate large amounts of normal pasteurised milk, but are able to tolerate cheese and yoghurt. Primary lactose intolerance presenting in infancy is rare and most infants having issues with dairy are likely to be diagnosed as being cow's milk allergic, not lactose intolerant. Secondary lactose intolerance, is transient and occurs when a child has had diarrhoea for example after a gastro bug which may result in the temporary reduction of the enzyme lactase. This leads to the poor absorption of lactose when consumed. This is usually resolved after a couple of weeks of a low-lactose diet. Both forms of lactose intolerance are different from being allergic to dairy and do not involve the immune system.

Most products that are lactose-free still contain cow's milk protein and are therefore not suitable for dairy allergy sufferers.

Dr Helen Cox

IF YOUR BABY IS NOT ALLERGIC TO DAIRY

Dairy is a key food group that should form part of your child's diet if your child's doctor has not told you to eliminate it. It is important to give your baby plenty of dairy products in addition to their formula or breast milk. It is full of protein, calcium and good fats and is an important part of your baby's and, later, toddler's diet. Good sources of dairy products for babies are yoghurt and cheese. Skimmed or semi-skimmed milk or low-fat yoghurts and cheese aren't a good idea, as your baby needs all the fat and nutrients found in the full-fat varieties.

Until babies are over one year old they should not have cow's milk as their main milk, and should stick to formula or breast milk instead. Cow's milk doesn't contain the right balance of nutrients your baby needs, though it is fine to use in cooking. At the bottom of many of our recipes we recommend adding milk, cheese, natural yoghurt, soured cream, crème fraîche, butter or cream for those babies and children who can have dairy products.

A NOTE ON SOYA

At least half of children with delayed reactions (non-IgE-mediated allergy, see page 12 for more information) to dairy will also react to soya milk and therefore soya milk is not a suitable milk replacement in this group of children. Conversely, the majority of children with immediate dairy allergy, like Ellie's daughter Isabelle, will tolerate soya milk and soya products, which can be a very useful addition to their diets after the age of six months. Your doctor or dietitian will be able to guide you as to whether soya milk can be tried.

Unlike most of the other dairy-free, non-formula milks, soya has similar levels of protein to cow's milk and relatively high levels of fat, which makes it a good replacement for cow's milk provided your child is free of tummy problems. The fortified varieties make a valuable contribution to your child's calcium intake but it's worth being aware that organic varieties are not fortified (as any supplements affect their organic status) so are not suitable.

Dr Helen Cox

EGGS

Eggs, like gluten, play a key role in baking, and can be found in a surprising number of foods where they aren't immediately obvious (see the chart on page 20). If your child is only allergic to egg, it is possible to make ordinary cakes using an egg replacement, and generally you can achieve good results. If your child has multiple food allergies, have a look at our birthdays section and our Puddings and Sweet Treats chapter for delicious cake and biscuit recipes that are free from major allergens.

Egg allergy is very common among children and, as with dairy allergy, many outgrow their allergy to egg in childhood. All birds' eggs from hens, ducks, geese or quails, for example, should be avoided by children with egg allergy. Raw egg is the most allergenic form of egg, followed by cooked egg and finally processed egg within foods such as cakes. There are many babies who are allergic to eggs in any form, including Isabelle and Casper, so all our recipes completely exclude eggs.

IF YOUR CHILD IS NOT ALLERGIC TO EGGS

Eggs are a useful source of both protein and iron. Until your baby reaches the age of one, eggs need to be well cooked to reduce the risk of food poisoning. Hard-boiled eggs, well-cooked scrambled eggs (both the white and yolk should be set) or well-cooked omelettes make a quick and easy meal. You can also use them for baking, of course.

PEANUTS AND TREE NUTS

Allergies to peanuts and tree nuts are distinct. Peanuts are often called ground-nuts as they grow underground and are part of the legume family. Brazil nuts, hazelnuts, pistachios, cashew nuts, pecan nuts, walnuts, macadamia (Queensland) nuts and almonds are all tree nuts. It is possible to be allergic to peanuts and not tree nuts, and vice versa. It is also possible to be allergic to just some tree nuts and not others. If this is the case for your child you need to carefully manage the risk of cross-contamination, as different types of nut are often processed in the same factory.

Many products carry warnings about traces of nuts – more so than other allergens.

It is worth noting that baby massage, which can be a popular activity for a mum with a small baby, often uses oils which are nut-based (sweet almond oil or macadamia nut oil, for example).

IF YOUR BABY IS NOT ALLERGIC TO NUTS

No child should eat whole nuts before the age of five due to the risk of choking, but if your doctor advises that your baby can eat tree nuts, peanuts or both, it is possible to offer nut butters such as peanut butter, almond butter or cashew butter on bread or toast. It is also possible to grind nuts up in a food processor or with a pestle and mortar to a powder, and mix the ground-up nuts into suitable yoghurts or puddings.

SOYA

Soya is relatively easy to avoid in day-to-day cooking but is commonly found in ready-made foods, as Fiona discovered when Casper had to cut soya out of his diet. Bread often contains soya so do check labels to find a brand that doesn't. Many other ready-made products and oriental foods (see the chart on page 20) contain either soya, or soya lecithin, or both.

Soya lecithin is a fat that is often used as an emulsifier and contains only trace amounts of the protein that causes allergic reactions. Many people with soya allergy are able to tolerate soya lecithin and, if so, there will be many processed and manufactured foods that they will be able to eat. You need to establish with your baby's doctor or dietitian if your baby (and you, if you are breastfeeding) can have foods containing soya lecithin.

IF YOUR BABY IS NOT ALLERGIC TO SOYA

Many children who are allergic to dairy are also allergic to soya; there is a high level of cross-reactivity, as the proteins found in both are similar (see page 25 for more information). However, if your child is allergic to dairy but can have soya, it can be a very useful part of your child's diet. There are many soya products available in supermarkets such as 'yoghurts', puddings, 'milk' and tofu, and they contain protein, energy and fat. All babies should have breast milk or formula for the first year of life, and after this many with dairy allergy continue on with hypoallergenic formula or breast milk for some time. However, if your child needs to move on to an alternative to cow's milk, fortified soya milk is a good option if there is no soya allergy. It has similar levels of protein to cow's milk, relatively high levels of fat, and those varieties fortified with calcium offer similar calcium levels to cow's milk (unfortified soya milk contains just a quarter of the calcium). We have several recipes that suggest adding soya if your child is not allergic.

GLUTEN

Gluten is found in cereals such as wheat, barley, rye, spelt and kamut. In addition, oats, because of the way they are produced, are generally cross-contaminated with gluten. Gluten is present in so many everyday foods, such as bread and pasta and plays a key role in baking cakes and biscuits. It can therefore be daunting when you need to cut it out of your baby's diet.

However, as Fiona found, once you get into the swing of things, it is straightforward to cook without gluten and there are also many off-the-shelf gluten-free products such as pasta and bread to make your life easier. Many gluten-free options do contain other allergens such as egg and dairy. Lupin flour is sometimes used to replace the wheat flour, so you will need to check labels carefully if your baby has multiple food allergies.

IF YOUR BABY IS NOT ALLERGIC TO GLUTEN

You can introduce bread into your baby's diet from six months. Be aware that there is often a lot of salt and sugar in bread, so check labels carefully. The same is true of breakfast cereals (even those aimed at children), but it is possible to find low-salt and sugar versions, and both bread and cereals are commonly fortified with nutrients such as iron and calcium and a range of vitamins so are an excellent part of a balanced diet. See page 37 for guidance on wholegrains.

According to European labelling guidelines, for a product to call itself 'gluten- free' it must contain no more than 20 parts of gluten per million. If a product states it is 'very low gluten' it can contain no more than 100 parts of gluten per million.

COELIAC DISEASE

This is not a food allergy but a genetic autoimmune disorder in which the protein gluten triggers an abnormal response by the body's immune system. The friendly fire from the immune system can damage the lining of the small intestine, affecting the absorption of food and potentially causing a range of problems including abdominal pain, diarrhoea, poor growth, poor weight gain, anaemia and malnutrition. Removing gluten from the diet allows the intestinal lining to repair and the gut to function normally. Coeliac disease needs to be managed with a strict gluten-free diet for life.

Dr Helen Cox

SESAME

Sesame is used fairly extensively in a variety of foods, especially in Indian, Greek, Chinese, Japanese and South East Asian cuisines. Something you come across all the time is hummus, which contains tahini – a paste made from sesame seeds. We have found that people seem to be less aware of sesame allergy. As Izzy is allergic to it, we find it invaluable that it needs to be highlighted on labels and in restaurants alongside the other major allergens.

We have a recipe for a delicious Red Pepper and Chickpea dip (see page 114) that is free from sesame and similar to hummus, which goes well with cucumber, carrots, peppers and other raw or cooked vegetables.

IF YOUR BABY IS NOT ALLERGIC TO SESAME

Sesame and tahini contain calcium, so hummus can be a useful addition to your child's diet, especially if your child is allergic to dairy. Hummus is also really nice for dipping carrots and other vegetables into. If your child can have sesame, you can add tahini to our Red Pepper and Chickpea recipe (see page 114). Sesame seeds can easily be sprinkled on almost any of our Flavour Combinations and can add an interesting new texture when your baby is ready for it. You can also add them to any Early Meals and Mini Meals that you like. They are particularly good on Asparagus Spears (see page 61), Vegetables in Coconut Cream (see page 146), Herby Chicken Dippers (see page 152) and Orange and Lemon Pork (see page 168).

FISH

There are many different types of fish and all of them are capable of causing an allergic reaction. Some people may be able to tolerate some types of fish and not others, but this must be established with a doctor. Even if this is the case, risk of cross-contamination is high all along the supply chain from when the fish are caught, through the transportation process, to when they are displayed alongside each other on the fish counter.

Omega-3 fatty acids are essential oils that should form part of every diet and the most common and complete source is oily fish. The oils are important for brain and eye development. Alternative plant sources such as flaxseed (also known as linseed) offer one type of omega-3, but oily fish is the best source of the whole range of oils and are easier to absorb than those from plant-based sources. Talk to your child's dietitian about omega-3 oils from fish oil, plant seed or sea algae supplements. The proteins that those with fish allergy react to are not typically found in well-refined oil, though they may contain traces.

IF YOUR CHILD IS NOT ALLERGIC TO FISH

Fish, including oily fish such as mackerel, salmon, fresh tuna, sardines, pilchards and many more is an important and valuable part of a varied diet. Fish is something you should aim to give to your child one to two times a week. Look for variations to our recipes - many chicken recipes provide suggestions for fish alternatives if your child is not allergic to fish, and some vegetarian recipes give options for adding fish as well.

You can also give your child tinned fish such as mackerel, pilchards, salmon or sardines if you crush any bones; they provide extra calcium, which is great especially if your child can't have dairy. Avoid fish tinned in brine, as this is very salty, but there are versions tinned in sunflower oil, olive oil or tomato sauce that contain less salt. Fresh versions of the fish are also easy to prepare and don't contain salt. Tinned tuna loses its essential oils in the canning process, so is not a source of omega-3. It's also worth noting that smoked salmon and smoked mackerel are high in salt and nitrates, so it's better to give your baby the fresh versions whenever you can. Large predatory fish such as swordfish are not suitable for babies due to potentially high levels of pollutants including mercury.

MOLLUSCS AND CRUSTACEANS

Shellfish should not be given to any babies under one year of age, according to the Department of Health, regardless of food allergy. We have included some information here about shellfish for completeness, as both molluscs and crustaceans are major allergens, and prawns and mussels and various other shellfish may be things you'd like to give your child as he or she gets older as part of a varied diet. Have a look at the chart on page 21 for foods that sometimes contain shellfish.

CELERY

Foods can contain different elements of celery, from the stems, leaves and seeds, and are also found in various spices, and celery salt. Celeriac is closely related to celery and should be avoided by those who are allergic to celery. Take a look at the chart on page 21 for information on foods that contain celery.

MUSTARD

When we think of mustard, jars of mustard come to mind. These are made up of ground mustard seeds mixed with other ingredients such as oil and vinegar. However, mustard can also be found in other forms such as mustard leaves. Like lupin allergy, it is a more common allergy in France and mainland Europe.

LUPIN

The lupin plant is part of the legume family, alongside peanuts and peas, and there is not a high incidence of lupin allergy in the UK. Lupin seeds or beans can be crushed to make lupin flour, which can be used in baked goods. It is commonly used in France and other countries in mainland Europe but is less usual in the UK. It is worth noting that some gluten-free products use lupin to replace more common gluten-containing grains, so you may find gluten-free products that don't contain wheat flour but contain lupin flour instead.

SULPHITES

Allergy to sulphites is rare and has key differences to other food allergies, but we have included some information on it here for completeness as it is one of the EU's official major allergens.

Sulphites are food additives used as preservatives and they are found in many kinds of dried fruit, particularly tree fruit (apricots for example) and also in cured meats such as ham and bacon. Ham and bacon are heavily processed and usually contain high levels of salt, so when our children were babies, we didn't give them any. As your children get older, you may choose to introduce these items sparingly as part of a varied diet. All our recipes exclude sulphites, and we haven't made suggestions for adding them.

ESSENTIAL NUTRIENTS

It is easy to give your baby a good start in life with a healthy nutritious diet. If you make a lot of home-cooked food from scratch (which is usually the case when catering for allergies) with plenty of variety, you can be confident you are giving your allergic child a balanced, nutritious diet through their food and, of course, their usual milk.

We have designed our recipes to make not only really tasty baby food and toddler meals, but also to use a wide variety of different vegetables, fruits, legumes, lentils and pulses – and a range of meats. This will ensure you are able to offer your baby a broad range of foods comprising protein, carbohydrates, fats and fibre (macronutrients) which contain a wide variety of vitamins and minerals (micronutrients).

In the early stages of weaning your baby's breast milk or formula will be providing the bulk of all necessary nutrients, but as your baby grows, he or she will need to get nutrients from food. Most of our recipes, particularly from Flavour Combinations through to Early Meals and Mini Meals, provide a complete and balanced meal or make serving suggestions (for example to serve with vegetables or rice or potatoes) if all the food groups are not part of the main recipe.

When your child has a food allergy you need to strictly avoid certain foods and even food groups, so don't forget that your baby and child's dietitian can give you much more detailed, specific advice about your child's individual diet, taking into account limitations presented by food allergy to ensure your baby is getting everything he or she needs.

PROTEIN is required for cell growth, tissue repair and immune function. Our bodies break down protein into smaller compounds known as amino acids. There are some amino acids that your body can manufacture (non–essential amino acids) and others that it needs to obtain from foods (essential amino acids). This is why it is really important to give your baby some form of protein in most meals. Meat (and fish if your child is not allergic to it) are the best forms of protein, as they contain all the essential amino acids. Non-meat sources such as pulses, seeds, soya and nuts contain some, but not all, amino acids and often in lower levels. Quinoa, a gluten-free, grain-like seed, does, however, contain a complete range of amino acids. Although it has lower levels than meat, it is still good news for those with allergies who can't eat some of the other non-meat sources of protein. We use quinoa in quite a few recipes in this book.

CARBOHYDRATES are the body's source of fuel, giving it energy. They come in the form of slow-releasing or 'complex' carbohydrates, or refined 'simple' carbohydrates. Babies and little ones certainly use up a lot of energy so, for those with allergies, it is fortunate that there is a good choice of carbohydrates, including rice and potatoes, which you can serve in an endless variety of ways.

FATS are an essential part of babies' and toddlers' diets. They provide energy, are critical for nervous system development and transport some vitamins around the body. A baby should not be on a low-fat diet. In fact, almost 45 per cent of the energy from breast milk comes from fat. Babies and toddlers will therefore need to eat some form of fat every day. It is easy to be bamboozled by nutritional terms but the best sources of healthy fats including omega oils are oily fish such as salmon, trout and mackerel. If your child is not allergic to fish it is a good idea to include this in their diet at least once a week. If your baby is allergic to fish, there are good plant-based options such as flaxseed oil, avocados, olive oil, rapeseed oil and coconut oil some of which are in our recipes.

FIBRE is the carbohydrate that cannot be digested by our body. It does not really provide any useful nutrients or energy, but it is vital for gut health. It is recommended that babies under the age of one year should not have wholegrain foods but you can introduce some wholegrain foods once your baby is over 12 months. (See page 37 for more information on introducing wholegrains to babies, toddlers and older children.)

PROBIOTICS

Probiotics play a pivotal role in the development of the immune system and it has long been considered that supplementing with probiotics may have health benefits. They are friendly bacteria often found in live yoghurts milk-based drinks and in some infant formulas. Dairy-free options are commonly available in powder and capsule form. They are able to colonise and restore the gut microflora. There is growing support for the use of probiotics in the prevention and treatment of eczema and in the treatment of gastroenteritis and antibiotic associated diarrhoea. It is, however, important to choose a probiotic that is not sensitive to any antibiotic that is being used, so speak to your child's doctor.

PREBIOTICS

While probiotics introduce good bacteria into the gut, prebiotics act as a fertilizer for helping the good bacteria grow. Arguably these can be at least as useful as probiotics and you don't need to introduce a supplement to your child's diet. Good sources are bananas, tomatoes, onions, Jerusalem artichokes, leeks and garlic. Look out for recipes that include these ingredients.

WHICH ALLERGENS TO AVOID

This book is designed for babies who have been diagnosed as food allergic or intolerant by a doctor. You obviously need to eliminate the food that your baby is allergic to and that your doctor has advised eliminating from your baby's diet. This is easy with our recipe book as it excludes all the EU's 14 major common allergens. You need to take advice from your baby's doctor about other allergens that your baby doesn't currently test positive for that are more likely to be a problem for your baby and should either be avoided or introduced with caution. Your baby's doctor or dietitian can provide advice on when and how often to introduce new foods and symptoms and reactions to look out for, and how to keep a record so you can identify any potential allergens that are causing a problem.

We realise it would be very unusual for your baby to be allergic to all 14 major allergens, so we have made suggestions where you can add foods such as fish, cheese, cream, butter, yoghurt, egg, tofu, crushed nuts or soya milk into the meals if your child is not allergic to them and your doctor has advised you to introduce them as normal.

FOODS ALL BABIES SHOULD AVOID UNTIL THE AGE OF ONE – REGARDLESS OF ALLERGY

- Honey (which can contain harmful bacteria)
- Unpasteurised cheeses (due to potentially harmful bacteria)
- Liver and liver pâté (due to very high levels of vitamin A which could be harmful to a baby)
- Whole nuts (due to choking risk)
- Tea and coffee (due to caffeine and interference with absorption of iron)
- Shellfish (which can contain harmful bacteria)
- Large predatory fish such as swordfish and marlin (due to potentially high levels of mercury)
- Added salt – there is no need to add any to food

SUGAR

Children who get used to a lot of sugar at a young age are arguably more at risk of eating unhealthy high-sugar diets at a later age, which can lead to numerous health problems. Sugary drinks and sugary foods such as cakes, biscuits, ice cream, ice lollies, lollipops and sweets can lead to tooth decay as well. It's important to note that foods we consider healthy like breakfast cereal and yoghurts – particularly those aimed at children – can contain surprisingly high levels of sugar so if you can, pick a brand that has less. For more information on sugar see page 184.

WHOLEGRAINS AND VERY HIGH-FIBRE FOODS

We're used to hearing that wholegrains and high-fibre diets are good things and that refined white versions of foods are not good for us, as they contain relatively fewer nutrients. It is useful to know that the advice for babies younger than 12 months is that they should avoid wholegrain pasta, bread (regardless of food allergy) and brown rice and should be eating the white versions instead. Current evidence indicates that babies need energy-dense foods, and that too much fibre fills them up without providing sufficient energy and too much fibre can also affect the absorption of vitamins and minerals. Once your baby is one, you can start slowly introducing some wholegrain versions as part of a broad diet, but guidance from the UK's Department of Health says that children shouldn't exclusively eat wholegrain versions of starchy food before the age of five.

SALT

Children should eat a lot less salt than adults, and babies and toddlers in particular should have none added to their food. If you are cooking at home for your baby you will know you are not giving them any added salt in food, so it's not a problem to give your baby things like bread and cereal which sometimes do have high levels of salt and sugar. But it's worth being mindful of other foods such as tomato ketchup, ham, smoked fish, crisps, supermarket soups, ready-meals and baked beans that are often popular with toddlers.

Stock cubes can also be high in salt, so have a look at our homemade stock recipes on pages 180–181. It's also worth noting that you can buy very low-salt stock cubes that are suitable for babies, but remember to check for allergens.

As a guide, babies should have less than 1g of salt per day. Many of our recipes have fresh herbs and other lovely flavours that mean you do not need to add salt to enhance the taste.

2

Weaning

BEFORE YOU START

As mothers ourselves, we know that life becomes easier once your baby can eat the same food as the rest of the family, meaning you don't have to cook separately. The recipes in this book – from First Tastes to Mini Meals – are therefore designed to get your baby and toddler ready to join the rest of the family eating a wide range of foods.

SAFETY

It's very important that you never leave babies alone at mealtimes, as they can choke. Always stay close to your baby when he or she is eating and make sure your baby is sitting upright and safely strapped into a suitable seat.

ROUTINES

We appreciate that everyone does things differently and the fact that your baby has a food allergy shouldn't affect this. You may be following a strict routine, or you may let your baby decide when they eat and sleep, or something in between. When our children were babies Ellie liked having a routine while Fiona was more laissez-faire, and we've both ended up with children who are pretty good eaters and sleepers. We have put together some meal planners to give you a guide as to when and what to feed your baby (see pages 220–227). You can, of course, adapt them however you like to suit you and your baby.

STARTING WEANING

Currently the World Health Organization suggests that weaning should occur ideally around six months of age to promote exclusive breastfeeding until this point. After six months the stores of iron and other nutrients that your baby is born with start to run out, and they need to be provided through solid food as they are not present in breast milk so the British Department of Health's advice is to wean at six months.

With regard to reducing the risk of developing food allergies, all international bodies suggest that weaning should occur between four and six months of age. It is important to note, that weaning should not occur before 17 weeks of age and not after 26 weeks of age, as doing it too early or too late have both been associated with an increased risk of developing allergies. There are many studies taking place at the moment looking specifically at this window of opportunity for introducing solids, so you may find that the advice will change in the years to come. It is therefore important to discuss this with your healthcare professional, to get the most up-to-date information on weaning for your child.

You may well have started weaning your baby already, and discovered an allergy when he or she ate a particular food. This was the case for both of us. If you have already started weaning your baby and your baby has now seen a paediatric allergy specialist, you can skip to the appropriate recipe section for your baby's stage.

If you are about to start weaning, you can work from the beginning of the recipe sections. If you are starting before six months, we suggest you give your baby more of the early recipes in the First Flavours and Flavour Combinations sections, before moving on to Protein Combinations. You will need to purée the meals well until this point, as baby-led weaning or finger foods are not recommended before six months. Go to the chart overleaf for more information on finger foods and textures of purée recommended at different ages.

WHEN TO WEAN

In summary the advice is never to wean before four months (17 weeks), and not to wait beyond six months (26 weeks). Start weaning when your baby is developmentally ready and showing signs of not being satisfied with breast milk or formula feeds.

PREMATURE BABIES

The advice on when to start weaning premature babies is somewhat different. Premature babies will typically be weaned when they are 6 months old (actual age calculated from date of birth rather than corrected age). When you wean will vary depending on how premature your baby was as you and your baby's doctor or health visitor will need to balance your baby's developmental stage with his or her need to have nutrients from solid food. Ellie's younger daughter was born at 31 weeks and she was weaned when she was just over six months old, although her corrected developmental age was four months. Babies born earlier may be weaned before they reach a corrected age of four months. The charity Bliss provides lots of useful information on weaning a premature baby.

WEANING STAGES

AGE	RECIPE SECTION	TIME OF DAY
17 WEEKS–26 WEEKS	First Flavours, Flavour Combinations (but not Protein Combinations).	One meal around mid-morning or lunchtime to fit with your baby's routine.
6–7 MONTHS	First Flavours, Flavour Combinations, including Protein Combinations as your baby approaches seven months. If you weaned your baby before six months you can introduce Protein Combinations from six months.	Initially one meal around mid-morning or lunchtime to fit with your baby's routine. Then introduce a small snack such as fruit or a First Flavour option at teatime once you are a couple of weeks into the weaning process and your baby is happy.
7–9 MONTHS	Flavour Combinations and Early Meals.	At this point you can introduce breakfast as well as tea so you build up to three meals a day. In addition, aim to introduce two courses at lunch and teatime. You can also add snacks in between meals to help boost energy.
9–12 MONTHS	Early Meals and Mini Meals.	By now your baby should be established on three meals a day, eating a wide range of food plus additional snacks as needed throughout the day.
12–18 MONTHS	Mini Meals and meals you are cooking for the rest of your family (free from your baby's allergens and salt of course).	Three meals a day and a snack of fruit or vegetables.
18 MONTHS +	Favourite Mini Meals and new recipes from *The Allergy-Free Family Cookbook*.	

TEXTURE	USUAL MILK
Finely puréed so texture is soft and smooth. Finger food is not recommended before 6 months of age.	Four to five full breastfeeds or 650–900ml formula.
Finely puréed if you're just starting weaning, moving on to small, soft lumps towards seven months. You can introduce soft finger foods such as cooked carrot, parsnip and butternut squash straightaway from six months as well as things like rice cakes or crunchy corn and quinoa cakes to add a variety of texture. You can vary serving hot and cold food so your baby gets used to these sensations.	Four to five full breastfeeds or roughly 650–900ml formula, reducing to four feeds and around 650ml formula as you introduce and establish solids. Your baby's milk will still provide the majority of nutrients, but as you establish weaning you will slowly start to cut your baby's breast milk or formula back in favour of solid food that will provide additional necessary nutrients such as iron.
You can purée more coarsely now or mash food, leaving bigger lumps. Continue with soft finger foods, and you can also introduce harder options such as breadsticks and pieces of meat for your baby to suck and chew on to introduce them to different textures. Soup also offers a new sensation.	Your baby's usual milk can now be cut back, but he or she should still be getting at least 600ml of formula a day or three breastfeeds a day, and he or she should be eating a wide range of foods including plenty of meat options for iron and protein.
If your baby is ready, many of these meal don't require mashing or blending but you can coarsely purée if you like. Many recipes offer texture through elements such as lentils and rice but are still easy for your baby to manage. Mini Meals do not need to be puréed or mashed.	Your baby should still be having 350ml* formula or three reducing to two breastfeeds a day. * Assuming your baby is having an additional 250ml of formula with breakfast cereal for example or sufficient dairy products like cheese to meet their daily calcium requirements.
Your child will need help cutting their food into small pieces as they get used to using cutlery (normally a spoon or baby fork to begin with).	350ml of formula or two breastfeeds (or cow's milk if your child is not allergic).
	Recommended milk as a drink from a beaker.

HOW MUCH?

For all babies, weaning will be messy. A lot of food will end up on the floor instead of inside your baby, and this is fine, especially when you are just getting started. It's important to let your baby guide you as to how much food to offer. Don't push it if your baby is not terribly interested to begin with or goes off his or her food a bit when teething, for example. Most of our recipes make enough food to purée effectively (too little and it's hard to blend), so any surplus can be frozen in small portions ready for future use. Each recipe gives you an idea of how much to offer your baby in a standard portion size, but this is intended to give you a rough sense of what to put in your baby's bowl rather than how much your baby will actually eat. If your baby wolfs it all down, you may want to offer a little more; equally, if he or she ends up eating just a small fraction of what you've offered, perhaps give less next time. Your baby may have as little as one or two spoonfuls to begin with, and this will be enough as a gentle introduction.

FINGER FOOD *or Purées?*

Almost all of our recipes can either be puréed or served as finger food for your baby to pick and choose from. When our children were babies we generally served puréed food, but with plenty of finger food on the side. It is very important to expose babies to a range of textures, encouraging them to try new things.

There are advocates of the spoon-feeding purée approach, and equally those who strongly believe in baby-led weaning, where a baby is able to pick and choose different whole pieces of food. We don't believe there is just one correct method, but rather that different approaches will suit different parents and babies – we think you should follow your instincts and find an approach that suits you. Our recipes will lend themselves to either baby-led weaning or spoon-feeding, or a mixture of the two.

We always tried to include our children in mealtimes when they were babies, and we think it's important for your baby to see you eat and enjoy your food; we often sit down together to eat as a family. It's particularly useful if your baby has an older sibling to sit with and to imitate at the table. We firmly believe that babies, and later on children, are more likely to try different foods if they see you and others eating a wide variety. When our children were babies we would often get together with friends who had babies of similar ages and feed them together – this was nice and sociable for us as well as them.

If you choose to purée and spoon-feed your baby, we recommend that you purée finely in the early days and then we suggest a coarser, lumpier texture as your baby gets the hang of eating – and don't wait too long to do this. A variety of textures is as important for your baby as a variety of flavours. Have a look at our chart on pages 42–43, which gives an indication of the type of textures you can expose your baby to at different stages and how that corresponds with our recipe sections. It's also a good idea to serve both hot and cold dishes so your baby gets used to the sensation of heat and doesn't favour one over the other.

The introductions to each recipe section and individual recipes themselves give guidance on texture if you plan to give your baby a purée, as well as how to serve finger food and most recipes are appropriate for both approaches. In the earlier recipe sections, we also often suggest making a purée but keeping some pieces whole to offer as finger food alongside the purée, as this is how we did things when our children were babies.

Your baby won't eat purées for ever. As they get older and you work through the recipe sections in this book, you'll find the meals no longer need to be blended and you can start to introduce more and more lumps and texture. Equally, if you are following a finger food approach, you may want to help your baby eat some of the non-puréed meals with a spoon. The aim of this book is to provide a breadth of recipes that help your baby go from early First Flavours through to Mini Meals, getting them ready to eat a range of foods with the rest of the family.

CHOKING

There is no evidence to suggest that finger foods are more likely to cause choking than purées, but you do need to be careful and consider the shape and texture of the food you are offering to your baby. Anything round like cherry tomatoes or grapes should be cut, as the whole pieces of fruit are slippery and can easily get stuck in the windpipe. Uncooked carrot and apple can be a problem, but if you cut them into slivers or grate them, they are less likely to present a choking hazard. Don't let your baby eat while on the move, whether playing or crawling. Food should be offered when your baby is sitting upright. The most important thing is never to leave your baby alone when eating, so you can react quickly. The thought of your baby choking is a frightening prospect, and if you haven't already done so, you may like to consider doing a first-aid course.

There is a difference between gagging and choking. When food gets near the back of the throat babies will gag, and the food will be pushed forward, often out of the mouth. Most babies gag when they are learning to eat and gagging is distinct from choking, when food goes down and gets lodged in the windpipe, preventing breathing.

LAYING THE FOUNDATIONS FOR HEALTHY AND UNFUSSY EATING

We believe all babies should be exposed to lots of interesting flavours and textures, and not be offered bland, boring food just because they are babies with allergies.

The more flavours, tastes and textures they're exposed to in the early days, the more likely they are to be prepared to try different things in the future. It is really important that your allergic child isn't a fussy eater, as his or her diet is likely to be limited by food allergy; if your child eats everything else, it will widen their choice significantly. We have suggested adding herbs and mild, aromatic spices to many of our recipes to bring out the natural flavours of the food. We have generally avoided mixing vegetables with fruit to sweeten them. We think it's a better idea to try and get a baby to like the true flavour of a vegetable rather than masking the taste. It's also worth persevering if your baby appears to reject a particular food. You can try some different things and return to the food they've turned their nose up at later. We've both found that our children's tastes are continually changing – things they loved as babies they are not always so keen on now, and things they didn't like before are now firm favourites – so don't take it as a given that your child will always reject a particular food that they're intent on spitting out at the moment. Try to avoid getting stuck in a rut serving the same five or six meals all the time (even if they do offer a completely balanced, healthy diet).

If your baby outright rejects a meal and you've made a big batch, pop the rest in the freezer and try again another time. We remember how frustrating this can be, but stick with it and don't get disheartened.

We know it's annoying when you've spent time cooking something lovely for your baby and then it gets rejected. We were advised not to move straight on to fruit, yoghurt or other puddings or snacks if our babies refused something, as this sends the message that your child can always get their favourite foods without bothering to try new or different things first. Hard as it is to let your child leave the table before they have eaten plenty, they will be getting most of their nutrients from breast milk or formula to begin with and it is perhaps better to have a few meals that are on the light side now and again that lead to your child eating a broad and balanced diet than to end up with a child who eats just a handful of things. We both know children like this who have very limited diets and it can be particularly worrying if your child also has food allergies.

Although food allergy can be daunting, it is important to try not to relay this anxiety to your baby. Both our children with allergies are on the slight side, and we always want to get them to eat plenty of high-energy and protein-dense foods and are conscious that we can sometimes be a bit pushy. This is almost always counter-productive. While we know this, we also appreciate it can be difficult to stop yourself! We realise it's hard, but try not to pressure yourself and keep mealtimes fun, relaxed and varied. Remember the big picture: if your baby or toddler doesn't eat a lot at one meal, they will probably make up for it at the next.

When you are feeding your baby and later sitting at the table with your children, try not to be distracted by reading or looking at your phone (we know we're guilty of this sometimes). Focusing on your baby and chatting to him or her, ideally while you are eating too, is a good way to encourage your baby to eat. Watching you and older children eating together and eating the same food is a perfect way to encourage your baby to enjoy meals and be prepared to try different things. Eating together is a fun, sociable part of our culture and we think it's great to introduce your baby to this as early as possible.

BREASTFEEDING MUMS

If you haven't started weaning your baby and you are breastfeeding, or if you are weaning your baby and still breastfeeding, your doctor and dietitian may have advised you to avoid foods to which your baby is allergic as some allergens can be passed through breast milk to your baby. Don't cut out foods while you are breastfeeding except on the advice of a doctor or dietitian. If your doctor *has* advised you to eliminate certain allergens from your diet, many of the recipes in this book can make a lovely meal for you, so you can cook for both yourself and your baby at the same time. Some of the purées can be made into delicious soups, and most of the Mini Meals – things like risottos, casseroles, bolognese and chicken dishes – are perfect for adults although you may like to add some seasoning. If your baby is in the very early stages of weaning you can always cook some of the later meals for yourself in large batches, eat some and freeze the rest – ready for when your baby is at the right stage for those meals.

If you would like even more variety, look out for *The Allergy-Free Family Cookbook*, which has more than 100 recipes to choose from.

PRACTICAL NOTES ON USING THIS BOOK

EQUIPMENT

You don't need to have elaborate equipment to make good baby food. We do however suggest some simple kit that we think will make things quicker and easier when preparing food for your baby, and to avoid cross-contamination. Many are items you will probably have already.

- **COLOUR-CODED CHOPPING BOARDS** – These are great for avoiding cross-contamination of foods. Such as raw meat and vegetables but you can use your own system to keep allergens apart.

- **KNIFE** – It's good to have a decent knife that's sharp and easy for you to handle. You will find you do lots of chopping when making baby food.

- **MEASURING SPOONS** – Not essential, but if you want to bake we think these are worth getting. Sometimes when baking – especially without eggs or flour – you need to be precise.

- **KITCHEN SCALES** – Electronic scales are inexpensive and very handy.

- **STEAMER** – A simple steamer for use on the hob is essential – steaming vegetables retains more nutrients than boiling.

- **BLENDER** – We like the handheld blenders that come with a couple of attachments. A little pot attachment is really handy for blitzing small quantities.

- **TUBS** – These are useful for keeping food sealed, fresh and away from any allergens you may have in the fridge or freezer.

- **FREEZER ICE-CUBE TRAYS** – These are handy for freezing small portions of baby food and you can cover them with a freezer bag. As your baby gets older you can use silicone muffin trays as you need larger portion sizes. You can also buy pots designed for weaning and these are handy when you're out and about.

- **HIGHCHAIR** – We like chairs you can push up to the table so your baby feels part of the family meal. However there are chairs with trays that are practical for containing mess. The most important thing is that the chair is stable and has a suitable harness and your baby can sit securely and upright in it.

- **BABY SPOONS AND BOWLS** – For young babies we used the rubber-tipped flexible spoons. Plastic bowls are useful as they will get knocked and tipped and banged on the table. As your baby grows, it's nice to let them try a baby fork that has short, blunt tines so your baby can spear soft food as well as scooping it up.

- **BIBS** – Feeding time can be messy, and using a plastic bib you can wash up or even put in the dishwasher saves additional laundry.

AVOIDING ALLERGEN CROSS-CONTAMINATION

Cross-contamination can happen easily but it is simple to keep food safe at home if you think ahead. Personally we don't have spreads like peanut butter in the house but we certainly do have other allergens that non-allergic members of the household eat. When preparing foods that contain allergens we are very careful where they are handled and ensure everything is cleared away carefully. Little children can be messy when eating, so when sharing a table with others eating an allergen you will need to take a few simple precautions:

- Use separate cloths to avoid spreading any allergens around the kitchen.
- Use separate spoons and knives for jams and spreads.
- Buy separate jars or tubs of spreads that no one else touches except for your allergic child/children.
- Keep an allergen-free shelf or section in the fridge.
- Buy a separate toaster for gluten-free bread.

- Sit allergic children opposite those eating allergens rather than next to them.
- Ensure everyone washes their hands well after eating or handling any allergens.

When you're out and about it can be a little harder to manage. Once babies are crawling and putting all sorts of things in their mouths, it can be difficult to keep an eye on them all the time and this can be a worry when they have allergies. We think it's important to find a balance between letting babies explore and keeping them safe from allergens.

At restaurants, ask staff to wipe down tray tables on highchairs, as they can often have dried milk or crumbs on them. You can buy small portable high chairs to avoid this. If you're travelling on a plane, wipe down tray tables and make sure your child doesn't put his or her hands down the sides of seats where debris including peanuts, crumbs and other allergens can accumulate.

COOKING TECHNIQUES
and Tips

All our recipes are straightforward, but we have a few tips to help you get the best results.

- **OIL** – Use a light olive oil or sunflower oil when cooking, and only use extra virgin olive oil in a cold state for salad dressings or enriching food once it's been cooked to add flavour. There are lots of different oils available so always check for allergens and to ensure they are suitable for heating to high temperatures if you are cooking with them.

- **ECHALION SHALLOTS** – Most of our recipes use echalion shallots rather than onions as they have a milder flavour than onions. They are readily available in supermarkets and are very easy to peel and chop finely. The ideal shallot is echalion, sometimes called 'banana shallot' because of its long, thin shape. You can of course use onion if you prefer, and it won't alter the taste of the dish significantly.

- **BROWNING MEAT** – Many of our dishes require you to brown meat, and this is a very easy skill to master and adds flavour to the dish, especially if you choose to use water rather than stock. Get the pan hot first and then add a little oil then put some of the meat in. Don't overcrowd the pan or the surface of the meat will not caramelise – it will start to sweat instead. Don't move it and let it take on some colour before you turn it. Ideally you are looking for a nice golden-brown colour, but not burned.

- **SWEATING VEGETABLES** – This method allows vegetables to become tender and flavoursome. In a frying pan or saucepan, with a little oil, allow them to cook and soften over a low to medium heat without browning.

- **MAKING FRESH STOCK** – Stock is really easy to make and definitely worth the effort. A lot of the stock cubes or fresh stocks that you can buy in supermarkets contain allergens such as gluten, egg and celery, and are often very high in salt. We tend to make a large batch and then reduce it down to a strong concentrate and freeze it in cubes. See pages 180–181 for two easy stock recipes.

- **VITAMIN DEPLETION** – It is worth noting that some vitamins such as vitamin C are depleted by cooking. The best sources of vitamin C are raw fruit and vegetables. For this reason we recommend serving crudités such as red peppers and carrots on the side at mealtimes when your baby is ready.

KEY TO THE RECIPES

As your baby or toddler is unlikely to be allergic to all 14 allergens, we suggest adding certain ones to recipes if your child is not allergic. It is important that your child's diet is not restricted more than necessary so look out for this icon at the bottom of recipes to see if there is an ingredient your child is not allergic to which you can add to the recipe.

If not allergic
Use soya milk for the cake for a different, slightly less airy, texture.

❄ Most of our recipes are suitable for freezing, so look out for this icon.

We give you a reminder to check labels of manufactured or pre-packaged ingredients that commonly contain allergens to ensure you buy a suitable brand.

3

First Flavours

When you start weaning the aim is to get your baby to have a taste and get used to the idea of solid food. It will be messy and often more food comes out than goes in. Remember – this is absolutely fine. Babies rely on breast milk or formula for nutrients and First Flavours are literally that – just little tastes and an introduction to the world of solid food; playing with food in their fingers and mouths is a good thing albeit very messy! Babies are ready for these First Flavours when they can sit up in a highchair and support their own heads, pick up food and manipulate the food in their mouths and swallow it (see pages 40–41 for more information on when to wean).

The First Flavours suggestions in this list all lend themselves to finger food or puréeing – whichever approach you prefer (or a combination, as we both did when we were weaning our babies). At this stage the purée texture should be soft and smooth, without lumps, particularly if you have chosen to wean before your baby is six months old. If you are weaning before six months you may want to offer more of these First Flavours than if you are weaning later and your baby is ready to move on more quickly.

Finger food is not recommended before six months but if you have started weaning when your baby is six months old you can serve these recipes either as a purée or finger food. We think all the foods on this list are good things to introduce your baby to before they move on to the combinations of foods in the next section. For allergic children in particular, it is useful to introduce just one food at a time to begin with so that if your child has a reaction you are able to pinpoint what has caused it. You can record your baby's responses to the food on our notes pages at the back of this book. You don't need to give your baby everything on the list – you can just pick and choose – but we would recommend making sure your baby gets plenty of vegetable choices as well as the fruit so they don't start off favouring the sweet options.

As well as providing a list of suggestions of early foods to let your baby try, we also make some suggestions as to how you can enhance the flavour once they've got used to the taste of the food on its own. For example, pea and mint is a lovely combination and there's no reason why a baby can't be introduced to flavours such as mint, coriander, parsley and cumin early on. We exposed our children to lots of varied foods and flavours when they were young, and we've found it relatively easy to introduce new foods later in life – they are generally prepared to give them a try (see page 48 for advice on raising an unfussy eater).

Rather than providing a list of instructions for how to purée, chop or mash different fruit and vegetables, this recipe section provides a list of foods that are good introductions to weaning your baby in the early stages and offer a nice range of First Flavours for your baby to try. These foods either don't need cooking at all, which makes life very easy or they can be steamed or baked. We'd generally recommend steaming rather than boiling, as nutrients are retained better. If your baby is reluctant to try food and is very fond of breast milk or formula, adding a little of that can make the new tastes a little more familiar to begin with. We found our children often weren't too keen on certain things on the first few occasions but on the third or fourth attempt really enjoyed the food and didn't look back. If your baby really won't eat certain things like broccoli or spinach that have a slightly bitter taste, you can try adding some butternut squash or sweet potato to reduce the intensity of the flavour. It is however important to persevere with these vegetables and evidence suggests that it can take a lot of attempts before some babies accept these flavours so don't give up too easily. Don't be tempted to mix these vegetables with fruit. If your baby can get used to the true flavour of vegetables from an early age, they will hopefully remain a popular part of your child's diet as he or she grows older. It's arguably more important for children with allergies to be unfussy eaters as their diets will be restricted so the more things they *will* eat from among the foods they *can* eat, the better.

After a week or two of trying these First Flavours, you and your baby will be ready to add in some ingredients and become more adventurous, moving on to the next recipe sections in this book safe in the knowledge that you have provided a solid basis from which to wean your baby in earnest.

YOUR BABY'S FEW FIRST TASTES OF SOLID FOOD

Give your baby solids between breast or formula feeds to ensure they aren't either starving or really full or you could even do it in the middle of a milk feed. Feed your baby a little of their usual milk to take the edge off their hunger, then some solids and finally finish off with the milk. You can then reduce the usual milk as solids increase. Choose a route to suit you.

The key when introducing solids is to create an environment in which your baby is receptive. To begin with make sure your baby is sitting in a suitable seat that supports them to sit upright. It may sound obvious but if you've chosen to offer a purée to begin with, place a little on a soft rubber-tipped spoon and gently put it between your baby's lips. Remember to smile and encourage your baby and make the experience a fun, pleasant one. Let your baby open their mouth. If there's no response, don't force the spoon but leave it a moment longer and perhaps put a little food on your baby's lip to lick off. If you are trying baby-led weaning or would like to offer finger food to begin with, lay some options in front of your baby to try. Whether you're offering finger food or purée, remember to let your baby guide you and decide when they have had enough.

After a few days or so, if your baby is happy eating solids and appears keen for more, you can increase the solid food slightly by adding another single taste at breakfast. Breast milk and/or formula should still be your baby's main source of nutrition (see the chart on pages 42–43).

This is a popular first solid food to give your baby as it has a simple taste, so when added to your baby's usual milk it makes a familiar first step into the world of solid food. You can also mix baby rice with puréed fruit or vegetables. Commercially prepared varieties that are fortified with nutrients like iron are available and if you're breastfeeding a fortified option may be a good idea. The iron stores your baby has laid down will be running low and your baby won't get iron through your breast milk. Both ordinary and hypoallergenic formulas are fortified with iron. In this recipe we use basmati rice as it has a delicate taste and is simple to prepare. Please note that your baby should not be having wholegrain rice or other wholegrain cereals at this stage (see page 37).

MAKES

30g

PREP: 5 MINUTES
COOK: 15 MINUTES

Homemade
BABY RICE

30g basmati rice
2–3 tbsp baby's usual milk

1 Boil the rice as per the instructions on the packet, and add a few extra minutes just to make sure that the rice is really well cooked and soft.

2 Drain and then push the rice through a sieve, the finer the better, using the back of a wooden spoon. Scrape the back of the sieve so you have all the rice in a bowl, then add your baby's usual milk.

3 Mix well with a small whisk until you have a thin, pasty consistency and serve immediately (see page 216). To make things a little more exciting you can add a little vegetable or fruit purée.

RIPE BANANA

This is a very easy first start. There is no preparation needed, which is always a bonus – especially as your baby probably won't eat a lot if it's the very first taste of solid food. You can mash it or give your baby some pieces to hold or do both. Ensure the banana is ripe; don't serve green, unripe bananas to babies as they can cause bloating and discomfort. Don't cut the banana into rounds if you are serving as finger food but rather into long chunks or batons, as it will be easier for your baby to hold and they are less likely to choke on it. Our children had banana as one of their very early tastes and it was a big hit with them all.

PEAR

Pears are easy to digest and gentle on little tummies. They have a sweet, delicately perfumed flavour that all babies seem to love and we think this is a great fruit to try in the very early days. Simply peel, remove the core and chop into slices that are easy for your baby to pick up and hold. Or you can blend into a purée.

SWEET POTATO

This has a nice vibrant colour and is slightly sweet so should be appealing as a first taste. Sweet potato has more energy than vegetables such as spinach or courgette so it can be a good option to begin with especially if you have a hungry baby. Just wash the skin and dry with a paper towel. Then bake in the oven like a jacket potato at 220°C/200°C Fan/425°F/Gas mark 7 for 40–50 minutes, or until it feels tender. Simply cut open, scoop out the flesh and allow to cool down. If it is a little dry, you can mix through some boiled water or your baby's formula or expressed breast milk to get to a smooth texture. As an alternative you can peel it and cut it into batons, steam it for about 12 minutes, until soft, and offer it as finger food.

CARROT

Carrots have remained a favourite with our kids and you can vary the flavour by adding a tiny pinch of cumin or a very small amount of fresh coriander once your baby has had them a few times. Peel, chop (in thick batons if serving as finger food) and steam the carrots for about 10 minutes until they're lovely and soft. If you choose to purée, you can add a little cooking liquid or your baby's usual milk.

BABY SWEETCORN

Steam baby sweetcorn for about 10 minutes until it's soft. If you choose to purée, you can add a little cooking liquid or your baby's usual milk.

ASPARAGUS SPEARS

Snap off the ends of the asparagus, as they can be a bit woody and stringy so not ideal for a baby. Steam the asparagus spears for about 8 minutes until they're lovely and soft. If you choose to purée, you can add a little cooking liquid or your baby's usual milk.

BUTTERNUT SQUASH

Butternut squash requires a little effort to peel, but does seem to be universally popular among babies because of its sweet taste, smooth texture and vibrant colour. Peel the butternut squash, dice or slice if serving as finger food. Drizzle with a little olive oil and bake at 220°C/200°C Fan/425°F/Gas mark 7 for 45 minutes, or simply steam for 15 minutes until it feels tender.

CAULIFLOWER

Cauliflower has a mild flavour and so it makes another good first taste. Little steamed florets make a nice finger food as they are very soft and easy for babies to eat, especially if you leave on some of the stalk for them to hold. However, you can also very easily mash or purée cauliflower. Simply break the cauliflower into small florets and steam for about 10 minutes, or until tender.

AVOCADO

Avocado is a lovely soft option and can be mashed or given as finger food (although it can be a little slippery!) Avocado is full of healthy fats and oils and is particularly good to include in the diet of a baby who needs to avoid dairy.

QUINOA FLAKES

If you have never cooked with quinoa (pronounced *keenwa*) before, do give it a try. It is a grain-like seed and is cooked in a similar way to rice. It is an excellent source of protein, containing all nine essential amino acids, so it is ideal for babies who are not ready to eat meat but still need high-quality protein in their diet. We'd suggest using quinoa flakes; these are seeds that have been rolled and they cook more quickly than ordinary quinoa and provide a softer consistency. Check the packet to ensure you get quinoa flakes rather than the ordinary quinoa seeds. Many varieties are organic. As well as protein, quinoa provides energy and is an easy ingredient to add to any First Flavours if your baby is especially hungry. We suggest simply cooking a small batch by following the directions on the packet and allowing it to cool. As it has a bland taste it will not mask any flavours you are introducing your baby to so you can simply add a teaspoon or more to any First Flavour recipe you are making. It is a good alternative to baby rice if you mix it with some of your baby's usual milk.

FRUIT

Fruit is a really important part of your child's diet. We've given you some options in this book to vary the fruit you offer your child, in the form of compôtes. Compôtes are essentially just purées that babies can have on their own when they're small. Compôtes also work well as accompaniments to other puddings when your child is older (fruit compôte goes well with the Rice Pudding on page 194, for example). Whole pieces of fruit are very good for your baby as they contain fibre, vitamins and minerals and most babies love eating them because they are naturally sweet.

Dried fruit contains higher levels of concentrated sugar. Although this is natural sugar rather than added refined sugar, whole pieces of fruit are a better option for your baby most of the time as they also contain fibre and water, so your baby is getting the sugar in the right, natural proportion. Dried fruit can be a convenient snack, but be mindful that your child will eat far more little raisins than they might grapes, and this can have an impact on their teeth. Some nutrients found in fresh whole fruit can be depleted in the drying process and dried fruit often contains sulphites, which are classed as a major allergen in the EU although reactions in children are very rare.

Fruit juices also contain high levels of concentrated sugar, and we would also recommend always giving your baby water rather than fruit juice. Again, fruit juice is missing the fibre, so your baby or toddler will end up having more and therefore a lot more sugar than in a whole piece of fruit. In addition, too much fruit juice can cause acid erosion to teeth. As much as possible we'd recommend giving your child pieces of fresh fruit.

You can give your baby almost any fruit (although we'd suggest being cautious about introducing kiwi fruit, as it is a relatively common allergen despite not being included in the EU's list of 14) and we have listed a selection to get you started. Making sure the fruit is ripe, you can either purée to whichever consistency suits your baby's stage and mix it with a little baby rice (see page 58) or quinoa flakes (see page 61), or serve it as finger food. Remember to consider the shape of the fruit, and ensure you slice up fruit like grapes and strawberries, which are round and can easily get lodged in your baby's windpipe. (See page 47 for more information on choking.) It's also worth remembering that fruit can be quite slippery so if you're offering it as finger food try to cut long pieces that your baby can clutch in a fist with a little piece sticking out of the top that can be sucked and chewed.

As your baby gets a little older you can introduce things like raspberries and strawberries that have seeds, and pineapple, but be sure to trim off any hard bits. It can be tempting to give your baby fruit all the time, partly because there's very little preparation for you and also because it's sweet so babies tend to wolf it down. But make sure you give them vegetables more often than fruit so they get used to different flavours. This is something that will stand them in good stead as they get older.

MAKES

3

PORTIONS

PREP: 5 MINUTES
COOK: 20 MINUTES

200g or 2 large dessert
 apples, peeled and
 core removed
1 strip unwaxed lemon peel
½ tsp lemon juice
1 tsp water

APPLE SAUCE

This apple sauce breaks down naturally to a soft consistency and doesn't need to be puréed. Make sure you
choose a nice sweet variety of dessert apple such as
Braeburn or Cox's, as cooking apples tend to be too sour.

1 Chop the apple into large chunks and put it in a pan with
the lemon peel, lemon juice and water. Cover with a lid and
cook over a low heat, stirring occasionally, for about 20
minutes, until the apple has broken down into a soft sauce.
Remove the lemon peel and leave to cool before serving.

MAKES

3

**GENEROUS
PORTIONS**

PREP: 3 MINUTES
COOK: 4 MINUTES

1 large ripe banana
½ tsp ground cinnamon

If not allergic

Add a small knob of
butter to the pan.

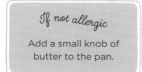
Bananas and CINNAMON

Bananas and cinnamon make a lovely combination.
Cinnamon is really versatile; it works well with both
savoury and sweet food, and tends to be popular with
children as it has a comforting, fragrant taste.

1 Cut the banana in half and then slice it lengthways so you
have little batons your baby can hold.

2 Put the sliced banana in a small frying pan over a low
heat, and sprinkle over the cinnamon.

3 Allow the banana to warm through and soften for
a couple of minutes before removing from the pan.

First Flavours **65**

PREP: 5 MINUTES
COOK: 5 MINUTES

APRICOT *Compôte*

200g fresh apricots, stoned
  and roughly chopped
  (or 410g tin of apricots,
  drained)
1 tbsp water (or juice
  from the tin)
1 tsp fresh lemon juice

This is great on its own or as an accompaniment to a suitable dairy-free pudding. It is also nice reduced down a little further to use on cakes under fondant icing instead of using jam. When apricots aren't in season, just use apricots tinned in juice instead.

1 Put all the ingredients in a pan and place a lid on top. Turn the heat up high. When the mixture starts to simmer remove the lid, turn down the heat a little and give it a good stir.

2 The apricots should break down very quickly, and within 5 minutes you should have a lovely apricot compôte. If you want a totally smooth compôte, simply blitz with a handheld blender. Allow to cool before serving.

PREP: 5 MINUTES
COOK: 10 MINUTES

STONE FRUIT *Compôte*

50g plums, stoned and
  cut into small pieces
50g peaches or nectarines,
  stoned and chopped
  into small pieces
50g blackberries, cut in
  half if large
1 thin strip unwaxed
  lemon peel
Star anise (optional)

This is a lovely accompaniment to our Rice Pudding (see page 194). The star anise gives a very gentle aniseed flavour, but you can leave it out if you prefer.

1 Place all the ingredients in a saucepan over a medium heat and allow the fruit to break down for about 10 minutes.

2 Allow to cool, remove the star anise and lemon peel before mashing or blending to the desired consistency, and serving.

MAKES

4

PORTIONS

PREP: 5 MINUTES
COOK: 10 MINUTES

Black Forest COMPÔTE

100g frozen or fresh
    black cherries
50g frozen or fresh
    seedless black grapes
50g frozen or fresh
    blueberries

We use frozen fruit when making this, as we find it breaks down very quickly, is widely available and is very easy to use; the stones and pips have been removed. If you wish you can use fresh fruit, but remember to remove the stones and pips and add a splash of water to the pan. This recipe is photographed on page 67.

1 Place a pan over a medium heat and add all the ingredients. Pop on a lid and bring to a simmer. Allow the fruit to cook for a few minutes.

2 Remove the lid and break down the fruit with a wooden spoon, and cook for a further few minutes.

3 Remove from the heat and purée with a handheld blender if you would like a totally smooth compôte. Allow to cool before serving.

MAKES

6

PORTIONS

PREP: 5 MINUTES
COOK: 8 MINUTES

Apple and Cinnamon COMPÔTE

300g dessert apples,
  peeled, cored and
  cut into pieces
¼ tsp cinnamon
2 drops vanilla extract

This is a really tasty pudding, and the vanilla gives it an extra hint of sweetness. Cooking apples can be a little bit tart, so we'd suggest using dessert apples such as Braeburn or Cox's. This recipe is photographed on page 67.

1 Put the apple into a saucepan and stir until it starts to soften and then totally breaks down to a soft consistency like a purée.

2 Add the cinnamon and vanilla extract and stir through. Allow to cool before serving.

4

Flavour Combinations

Once your baby has tried some of the First Flavours, you'll be ready to try some combinations. Our children really enjoyed these and they have been popular with our baby testers. In some recipes we have recommended adding herbs and spices, which enhance the natural flavours of the ingredients. We believe it's a good idea to introduce babies to some of these mild flavours early on. You can serve many of these combinations as finger foods if your baby is over six months old or blend them to a purée. And, if puréeing, you can vary the texture to suit your baby and start to introduce a few soft lumps. You can freeze most of these as purées and we suggest you make more than you need for one meal. It is difficult to blend very small amounts of food and it saves time to cook once and create several meals. If you are serving finger food you can simply reduce the quantities to make enough for one meal.

At this stage your baby should be happy eating from a spoon and picking up pieces of food. Hopefully your baby will also be looking forward to their solid food and getting excited or impatient as you are making it. This is when you can start to reduce the amount of breast milk or formula a little in favour of food (see the chart on pages 42–43). At breakfast time the main food should be your baby's usual milk, but you can add in a little bit of fruit as well. Remember, many vegetables and fruit – while containing lots of vitamins – don't contain much energy, so mixing green vegetables with things like sweet potato, butternut squash or quinoa flakes is a good way of giving your busy and active baby more carbohydrate.

At around the six-month mark, babies will start to run low on iron stores laid down at birth and will need to get this from their diet. Iron is an important mineral that is essential for making haemoglobin, which transports oxygen in the blood around the body to the organs and muscles. Iron is also important for brain development in babies and small children and it is found in two forms. Haem iron is found in sources such as red meat and dark chicken meat and is readily absorbed by the body. Non-haem iron comes from plant-based sources such as pumpkin seeds, lentils, chickpeas, kale, beans, broccoli and peas. The body finds non-haem iron harder to absorb but absorption can be improved with the help of vitamin C.

If you are exclusively breastfeeding it is essential that you give your baby iron-rich foods when you start weaning (formula milk, including specialist hypoallergenic formula, is fortified with iron). Initially you may not want to serve your baby meat so our recipes include plant-based sources of iron alongside vitamin C-rich ingredients: Roasted Parsnip, Carrot and Broccoli, see page 91; Carrot and Coriander, see page 94; and Cavolo Nero with Butternut Squash, see page 85. As your baby approaches seven months (or earlier) it is important that they start eating some meat, and you can introduce Protein Combinations such as Beef, Butternut Squash and Sweet Potato, see page 135.

Remember that at this stage your baby should still be relying on breast milk or formula as their main source of nutrition so ensure that they are not having so much solid food that they cut back too much on their usual milk.

NUTRITIONAL BOOSTS

You can boost the nutritional content of any of the recipes in this section by stirring in:

- 1 tbsp cooked quinoa flakes (a great source of protein).
- 1 tbsp cooked lentils (another good source of protein).
- A drizzle of linseed oil for babies (the ground flaxseed is too high in fibre for babies but can be given to toddlers).
- A drizzle of olive oil (a good source of unsaturated fat) at the end of cooking.
- A drizzle of rapeseed oil.
- A drizzle of pumpkin seed oil (a source of many minerals, including iron). Pumpkin seeds are too high in fibre for babies but crushed pumpkin seeds can be given to toddlers.
- Vitamin C-rich foods such as red peppers, pineapple or berries; vitamin C is heat sensitive, so ideally offer these raw.

OPTIONAL EXTRAS IF YOUR CHILD IS NOT ALLERGIC

- Hummus contains tahini made from sesame (a good source of calcium).
- A sprinkle of unsalted ground up nuts (a good source of vitamins and minerals, including calcium, omega 3).
- Nut butters such as peanut butter, cashew nut butter, almond butter.
- A knob of unsalted butter, grated cheese, soured cream, yoghurt or crème. fraîche (a good source of calcium, iodine and B12).
- A little chopped tofu (a good source of protein).
- A chopped hard-boiled egg (a good source of protein, fat, vitamins and minerals).

MAKES
2
PORTIONS

**PREP: 5 MINUTES
COOK: 50-60 MINUTES**

This is very easy as you can just pop a sweet potato in the oven to roast and forget about it while you get on with other things. The allspice just adds a little extra mellow flavour not dissimilar to cloves, cinnamon and nutmeg. It can be overpowering if you add too much so just add a tiny pinch.

SWEET POTATO
and Allspice

1 small sweet potato, washed
Drizzle of olive oil
Small pinch allspice (adjust to taste)

If not allergic

Add a knob of butter instead of the olive oil, and a little grated cheese.

1 Preheat the oven to 220°C/200°C Fan/425°F/Gas mark 7.

2 Pop the sweet potato on a baking sheet and in the oven to roast for about 50–60 minutes until it feels soft.

3 Remove from the oven and allow to cool a little before cutting it open and scooping out the flesh into a bowl. Add a drizzle of olive oil and the allspice, and stir really well.

4 Allow to cool a little further and serve.

Fiona's son Casper always used to call cauliflower broccoli's best friend and they certainly do go well together in this simple combination; the cauliflower softens the stronger taste of the broccoli. The carrot with its gentle sweetness brings them together to create this popular combination.

Cauliflower and
BROCCOLI

130g cauliflower, cut
    into florets
50g broccoli, cut into
    florets
50g carrots, peeled
    and chopped

If not allergic

Add a little cheese
at the end when
puréeing or serving.

1 Set a pan of water to boil over a high heat and place a steamer on top.

2 Add the cauliflower, broccoli florets and the carrot. Steam for about 7 minutes, or until the vegetables are tender.

3 Serve as finger food or mash or purée to serve, adding a little cooking liquid or your baby's usual milk if required.

PREP: 5 MINUTES
COOK: 15 MINUTES

Cabbage is a good source of many minerals and vitamins. It does not have a reputation for being the most exciting of vegetables but we think this is rather unfair, and urge you to cook with it for your whole family. Babies will enjoy this, as the sweet potato gives this purée a lovely smooth texture while the cabbage flavour comes through subtly.

SWEET POTATO
and Cabbage

1 tsp olive oil
300g sweet potato,
    peeled and chopped
    into small dice
150g white cabbage,
    shredded, avoiding
    the heart
300ml water

If not allergic

Sweat the vegetables
in a little butter
instead of olive oil.

1 Heat the oil in a saucepan over a low–medium heat, then add the sweet potato and cabbage.

2 Let the vegetables sweat for about 3 minutes, then add the water.

3 Bring to a simmer and cook for about 10 minutes, or until the vegetables are tender. Remove from the heat, and drain.

4 Purée, adding a little cooking liquid or your baby's usual milk, if required, to get to the right consistency.

MAKES

2

PORTIONS

PREP: 5 MINUTES
COOK: 50 MINUTES

Aubergines are great for babies, as they are so soft and tender when cooked and have a delicious subtle flavour. Combined with the courgette this makes a very simple purée with a lovely creamy texture. As the vegetables are oven roasted they intensify and develop a sweet taste. To make life easy, you can pop everything in the oven and get on with other things while it cooks. We recommend this recipe as a purée to get the most out of the creamy texture.

COURGETTE
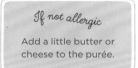
and Aubergine

1 medium aubergine
2 courgettes, chopped
   into chunks
1 tsp olive oil
1 garlic clove, skin on

If not allergic

Add a little butter or cheese to the purée.

1 Preheat the oven to 220°C/200°C Fan/425°F/Gas mark 7.

2 Put the whole aubergine in a roasting tin and bake. After 30 minutes add the courgettes and garlic clove, drizzle them with olive oil and cook for a further 20 minutes.

3 Remove from the oven and carefully cut the aubergine down the middle (it will be hot) and scoop out all the flesh. Put it in a bowl with the courgettes. Peel the garlic and add it to the bowl and mix together well.

4 Mash or purée to serve, adding a little of your baby's usual milk if required.

Roasting the red pepper and butternut squash makes a lovely sweet combination, as the flavours become concentrated and more intense. The vibrant red and yellow colours also look really attractive and appeal to babies.

Red Pepper and
BUTTERNUT SQUASH

330g butternut squash,
peeled and chopped
into small cubes
40g red pepper,
deseeded and sliced
1 tbsp olive oil

1 Preheat the oven to 220°C/200°C Fan/425°F/Gas mark 7.

2 Place the butternut squash and red pepper on a baking tray, drizzle with the olive oil and toss well, ensuring that all the pieces are coated.

3 Bake for 15 minutes, or until the butternut squash is soft. This may take longer if you have larger cubes. Remove from the oven and allow to cool.

4 Offer as finger food, or mash or purée to serve, adding a little of your baby's usual milk if required.

if puréed

PREP: 5 MINUTES
COOK: 20 MINUTES

Parsnip is a popular root vegetable that has loads of flavour. When roasted and combined with butternut squash it makes a smooth and comforting purée – perfect as an early introduction to solid food.

PARSNIP
and Butternut Squash

1 tsp olive oil

1 echalion shallot, peeled and chopped

300g butternut squash, peeled and cut into small dice

150g parsnip, peeled and sliced

300ml water

If not allergic

Stir in a teaspoon of either single or double cream or oat cream when serving.

1 Heat the oil in a saucepan over a medium heat and then add the shallot, butternut squash and parsnip and allow to sweat for about 4 minutes.

2 Add the water to the pan and allow to simmer for about 15 minutes, until the vegetables are tender and some of the liquid has evaporated.

3 Remove from the heat and drain, reserving the remaining cooking liquid. Blitz with a handheld blender and adjust the consistency to suit your baby, adding a little cooking liquid or your baby's usual milk if required.

MAKES

4

PORTIONS

if puréed

PREP: 5 MINUTES
COOK: 30 MINUTES

Roasted carrots are naturally sweet and are always a hit with little ones. The roasted garlic is mild in flavour so do give it a go. We like to purée most of the carrots but leave some whole for babies to pick up and eat themselves. Once you've finished cooking you can add a drizzle of olive oil.

CARROTS, GARLIC
and Parsley

350g carrots, peeled and chopped into batons
1 large garlic clove, left whole with skin on
1 tbsp olive oil
Small handful chopped fresh parsley

1 Preheat the oven to 220°C/200°C Fan/425°F/Gas mark 7.

2 Drizzle the carrots and garlic with oil in a roasting tin. Toss well ensuring all the pieces are coated. Place in the oven for about 30 minutes.

3 Remove from the oven and then squeeze the garlic out of its skin and stir to disperse it over the carrots, then scatter over the chopped parsley.

4 Mash or purée to serve, adding a little of your baby's usual milk if required.

MAKES
4
PORTIONS

if puréed

PREP: 5 MINUTES
COOK: 5–10 MINUTES

The spices added to the cauliflower are very mild, with no heat, so they simply add earthy aromatic flavours. You can of course increase the spices to taste, but we suggest adding the recommended amounts to begin with.

Cauliflower and AROMATIC SPICES

300g cauliflower,
    cut into florets
1 tsp olive oil
¼ tsp ground cumin
¼ tsp ground coriander
Small pinch turmeric

If not allergic

Add a little natural yoghurt, either mixed in or on the side.

1 Set a pan of water to boil over a high heat and place a steamer on top.

2 Add the cauliflower florets and steam for about 5 minutes, or until they feel tender.

3 Place the steamed cauliflower in a small saucepan over a medium heat and add the oil, cumin, coriander and turmeric. Stir well so the cauliflower florets are well coated and cook for a further minute, stirring gently.

4 Mash or purée to the desired consistency, if puréeing or serve as finger food.

PREP: 5 MINUTES
COOK: 10 MINUTES

Cavolo nero has very dark green, almost purple leaves and is a good source of iron for your baby. We have paired it with butternut squash to give a lovely smooth texture and some vitamin C to help with iron absorption. When chopping the leaves, do remove the stems as they can be quite fibrous.

Cavolo Nero with
BUTTERNUT SQUASH

60g cavolo nero, hard
    stems removed and
    leaves chopped
250g butternut squash,
    peeled and chopped
    into small cubes

1 Set a pan of water to boil over a high heat and place a steamer on top.

2 Add the cavolo nero and butternut squash. Steam for about 10 minutes, or until the vegetables are tender.

3 Purée to serve, adding a little cooking liquid or your baby's usual milk if required.

MAKES

3

PORTIONS

PREP: 1 MINUTE
COOK: 5 MINUTES

This is a really fresh combination, and very pretty with its vibrant bright green colour. Most children and babies we've come across like peas, and it's nice to introduce babies to them early. This also makes a really delicious adult soup if you add some chicken stock.

PEA AND MINT

250g frozen peas
   (petits pois are best)
3 or 4 mint leaves
Cooled boiled water,
   if needed

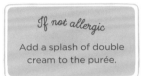

If not allergic

Add a splash of double
cream to the purée.

1 Set a pan of water to boil over a high heat and place a steamer on top.

2 Place the peas and mint in the steamer above the pan and put a lid on top. Cook for 3 minutes, or until the peas are cooked.

3 If you want to keep the bright green colour, plunge into cold water, then drain.

4 Blend with a handheld mixer (adding a little cooled boiled water or your baby's usual milk if you prefer a thinner consistency).

PREP: 1 MIN
COOK: 35–40 MINUTES

These are a great alternative to chips, and they also add a splash of colour to the plate. They are ever so simple to make and popular with all ages, not just babies and toddlers. These are also nice served with dips such as our Red Pepper and Chickpea (see page 114), and Avocado and Artichoke (see page 92).

SWEET POTATO WEDGES
with Dips

2 small sweet potatoes,
   washed and sliced
   lengthways into wedges
Drizzle of olive oil

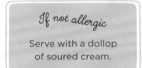

If not allergic

Serve with a dollop
of soured cream.

1 Preheat the oven to 220°C/200°C Fan/425°F/Gas mark 7.

2 Place the sweet potato in a roasting tin and drizzle over a little olive oil.

3 Bake for 35–40 minutes, until the wedges are tender.

VARIATION

Sprinkle over a little pinch of sweet smoked paprika when serving.

MAKES
4
PORTIONS

PREP: 10 MINUTES
COOK: 15 MINUTES

This cannot be puréed, as the potatoes will make a stodgy, wallpaper-paste consistency. When you mash it, it will have some little lumps, so it's great for babies who are ready for some texture. The courgette gives this recipe a delicious creaminess, but you can add in any extra vegetables you happen to have around.

MASHED POTATO
with Vegetables and Dill

1 tbsp olive oil, plus an extra drizzle
1 tsp echalion shallot, finely chopped
300g small potatoes, peeled and chopped into small pieces
100g courgette, peeled if preferred, and chopped
350ml water
40g frozen peas (petits pois are best)
Sprig dill, chopped

> *If not allergic*
>
> Add a little milk and butter when mashing.

1 In a saucepan heat the oil over a medium heat and add the shallot, cooking it has softened.

2 Add the potatoes and courgette to the pan, cover with the water and cook until the potato feels soft. This should take about 8 minutes. Add the peas and cook for a further minute.

3 Carefully drain the water into a bowl, and mash the vegetables using a potato masher, adding the reserved cooking liquid as needed.

4 Stir in the chopped dill and a drizzle of olive oil.

VARIATION

Add any other vegetables you like; parsnip, savoy cabbage and Brussels sprouts all work well. Simply chop them finely and add them with the potato. Parsnip will mash down nicely with the other ingredients. Cabbage or Brussels sprouts will add an especially good texture.

PREP: 5 MINUTES
COOK: 30 MINUTES

Roasting the parsnip and carrot makes this a flavourful baby meal that is also a source of iron, thanks to the broccoli. If you are puréeing you can add a few extra florets of broccoli to the steamer to have as finger food on the side.

Roasted Parsnip,
CARROT AND BROCCOLI

80g carrot, peeled and
    cut into batons
Drizzle olive oil
300g parsnip, peeled
    and cut into batons
50g broccoli florets broken
    into small pieces
4 tbsp cooled boiled water
    if needed

If not allergic

Add a little milk or
cream if puréeing.

1 Preheat the oven to 220°C/200°C Fan/425°F/Gas mark 7.

2 Put the carrots in a roasting tin and drizzle with the olive oil. Toss well to ensure all the pieces are covered. Bake, and after 10 minutes add the parsnips. Mix and bake for another 20 minutes. If they are not tender, leave for another 5 minutes and check again. When they are ready, remove from the oven.

3 Meanwhile, steam the broccoli for 5 minutes.

4 When all the vegetables are ready either allow to cool and serve, or purée to the desired consistency, adding some cooled boiled water or your baby's usual milk.

This purée can be eaten on its own but also makes a delicious dip for crudités and other finger food. It is quick, and there's no cooking required so is very easy to rustle up if you have a jar of artichokes in the cupboard and an avocado to hand.

Avocado and ARTICHOKE

1 ripe avocado
8 artichoke hearts from a jar, drained and rinsed

Label check
Check your jar of artichokes for any allergens.

1 Scoop out the flesh of the avocado, discarding the stone, and blend with the artichoke to the desired consistency.

VARIATION

A chopped deseeded tomato is a nice addition, stirred in for a bit of extra texture.

If not allergic

Add a little double cream or oat cream when blending.

PREP: 5 MINUTES
COOK: 10 MINUTES

This is particularly good served as a finger food, but you can also purée it. The carrots are delicious dipped into one of our other purées, such as Courgette and Aubergine (see page 78) or Butter Bean and Butternut Squash (see page 104) but they are also great on their own, as the coriander gives them a subtle citrus flavour. It's best not to let the carrots get too soft so your baby can really gnaw on them with their gums (or teeth, if some have already arrived).

CARROT
and Coriander

½ **carrot, peeled and cut into batons**
½ **tsp olive oil**
¼ **tsp ground coriander**

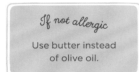

If not allergic

Use butter instead of olive oil.

1 Set a pan of water to boil over a high heat and place a steamer on top.

2 Add the carrots. Steam for about 5 minutes, or until tender.

3 Place the steamed carrots in a small saucepan over a medium heat and add the oil and coriander. Stir well so the carrots are well coated and cook for a further minute, stirring gently.

4 Allow to cool and serve.

PREP: 5 MINUTES
COOK: 50 MINUTES

This purée has both an earthy flavour and a vibrant colour. Beetroot is high in iron and other nutrients and is great to include in your child's diet. You do need to buy fresh beetroot, not the pickled variety that comes in packets or jars. It can stain your hands so wash them straightaway once you've peeled and chopped the beetroot.

Roasted Sweet Beetroot and
BUTTERNUT SQUASH

300g fresh beetroot,
   peeled and chopped
   into chunks
400g butternut squash,
   peeled and chopped
   into chunks
Drizzle of olive oil
Cooled boiled water,
   as required

1 Preheat the oven to 220°C/200°C Fan/425°F/Gas mark 7.

2 Put the beetroot and butternut squash in a roasting tin and drizzle with the olive oil. Toss well ensuring all the pieces are coated. Cover the tin tightly with foil and bake. After 50 minutes, check that the vegetables are nicely roasted and the flesh is tender when you prod them with a fork.

3 If they are not ready, leave for another 5 minutes and check again. When they are ready, remove from the oven.

4 Allow the vegetables to cool, serve or purée to the desired consistency, adding up to 4 tablespoons of cooled boiled water if necessary to create a smooth purée.

> *If not allergic*
>
> This is really good with some pasteurised soft goat's cheese.

PREP: 5 MINUTES

This combination is easy as no cooking is required, and it's very quick to put together. This cold soup is another sensation for your baby to try. There is a high water content in cucumber and tomatoes, so this is good on a hot day when you need to keep your baby hydrated. It can be sieved if you prefer to remove the seeds. We like to add cooked quinoa flakes to this recipe to make the meal more substantial.

GAZPACHO

10 cherry tomatoes

4 basil leaves

1 tbsp olive oil

⅓ cucumber

2 tbsp cooked quinoa flakes
   (optional)

1 Put the cherry tomatoes, basil, olive oil and cucumber in a jug and blitz with a handheld blender until smooth. If you like you can then sieve the mixture to make it completely smooth.

2 Add in the cooked quinoa flakes, if using.

If not allergic

Add little cubes of tofu or mozzarella cheese for additional protein and texture.

This is so easy, especially if you haven't had a chance to go shopping, as it uses tinned ingredients. We'd suggest using the 'no added salt or sugar' tins of sweetcorn. Ideally we would also suggest using either our Simple Vegetable or White Chicken Stock (see pages 180–181), as it gives an additional flavour, but water is also fine if you don't have any stock to hand. Do mash a little or purée, as chickpeas pose a choking hazard if left whole. As this recipe uses whole tins it makes a quite a lot but you can freeze what you don't need now to use another time.

MAKES

8

PORTIONS

PREP: 5 MINUTES
COOK: 15 MINUTES

Chickpea and
SWEETCORN CHOWDER

½ tbsp olive oil

1 echalion shallot,
    finely sliced

60g carrot, peeled and
    very finely diced

400g tin chickpeas,
    drained and rinsed

200g tin baby sweetcorn,
    drained and rinsed

500ml Simple Vegetable
    or White Chicken Stock
    (see pages 180–181),
    or water

Sprinkle finely chopped
    chives

Sprinkle finely chopped
    oregano

1 Put the oil in a large saucepan over a medium to low heat and then add the shallot and carrot. Allow the vegetables to sweat in the oil for a few minutes.

2 Add the chickpeas, sweetcorn, stock or water and herbs, if using, to the pan. Bring to a gentle simmer for 10 minutes, and then remove from the heat.

3 Mash or purée to the desired consistency.

If not allergic

Add a little
crème fraîche

PREP: 5 MINUTES
COOK: 15 MINUTES

Remember not to use a blender with potato, otherwise it will become a horrible gluey mess. You can mash this down to quite a smooth consistency with a potato masher, but it will have some little lumps which we think are great for introducing texture. The potatoes and peas soften the strong taste of the spinach to make this a tasty combination.

PEAS, SPINACH
and New Potatoes

200g new potatoes,
   washed and cut into
   small pieces
70g frozen peas
   (petits pois are best)
70g spinach, washed

1 Put the new potatoes in a saucepan of cold water and bring to the boil.

2 After 5 minutes, place a steamer on top of the pan, add the peas and spinach and cover with a lid.

3 After a further 5 minutes or so, take off the spinach and peas and blend, adding a little cooking liquid if needed. Drain the potatoes separately.

4 Using a masher, crush the new potatoes to the right consistency for your baby, add the blended spinach and peas and mix together.

MAKES
3
PORTIONS

PREP: 5 MINUTES
COOK: 15 MINUTES

It is always great to have a bag of frozen broad beans in your freezer as they offer a good source of vitamins and iron. The sweet potato gives the purée a nice smooth texture making this a winning combination.

BROAD BEAN, COURGETTE
and Spinach with Sweet Potato

120g sweet potato, peeled and cut into small cubes

75g courgette, cut into small cubes

30g fresh or frozen spinach

75g frozen or fresh broad beans

1 Set a pan of water to boil over a high heat and place a steamer on top.

2 Steam the sweet potato for 5 minutes.

3 Add the courgette, spinach and broad beans to the sweet potato and steam for a further 5 minutes.

4 Remove from the steamer and serve mashed or puréed, adding a little cooking liquid or your baby's usual milk to get the right consistency.

If not allergic
Add a little grated cheese.

PROTEIN COMBINATIONS

We have already mentioned the importance of including sources of iron in your baby's diet, especially if you are exclusively breastfeeding, and it's also great to introduce plenty of protein. You may not want to introduce them immediately if you started weaning at six months; you may prefer to try some simpler options first but these options are suitable from six months, particularly if weaning is already established. These recipes contain sources of iron and vitamin C where needed to aid iron absorption.

MAKES

4

PORTIONS

PREP: 5 MINUTES
COOK: 10 MINUTES

250g butternut squash, peeled and chopped into small pieces
80g tinned butter beans, drained and rinsed

If not allergic

You can add a little grated cheese.

BUTTER BEAN
and Butternut Squash

Butter beans are deliciously creamy and give this purée a beautifully smooth texture. They also offer a plant-based source of protein for your baby and it is very handy to have a tin of these in your cupboard.

1 Set a pan of water to boil over a high heat and place a steamer on top.

2 Add the butternut squash and steam for about 7 minutes, or until tender.

3 Remove from the steamer, place in a bowl and add the butter beans. Mash with a fork or blend to a purée as desired.

MAKES

4

PORTIONS

PREP: 5 MINUTES
COOK: 55 MINUTES

This is a very simple beef mince recipe that has a fairly smooth texture when puréed. If your baby is progressing well with the weaning process and you want to offer a coarser texture, you can purée just half of the recipe and mix it together with the rest.

Simple MINCED BEEF

1 tsp olive oil
160g beef mince
1 echalion shallot, peeled
 and finely chopped
90g courgette, peeled
 and finely chopped
60g carrot, peeled
 and chopped
250ml White Chicken Stock
 (see page 181)

If not allergic

Serve with a little
grated cheese.

1 In a heavy-bottomed pan, heat the oil over a medium to high heat, then add the beef mince and allow it to brown. Use a wooden spoon to really break up the mince and make sure there are no large clumps of meat, especially if you do not plan to purée the whole recipe.

2 Add the shallot and cook until it just starts to soften. Then add the courgette and carrot, and give everything a good stir.

3 Add the stock and bring to a gentle simmer. Cover and cook gently for 45 minutes.

4 Remove from the heat and purée to the desired consistency.

MAKES

4

PORTIONS

❄

PREP: 5 MINUTES
COOK: 35 MINUTES

If you can't get hold of spring greens then curly kale is a perfect substitute for this recipe. Packed full of vitamins and minerals, including iron, this really is a nutritious combination. Greens can be bitter and may be hard for a young palate to adjust to, but in this recipe the bitterness is counteracted by blanching the greens first and then adding the additional flavours of garlic, lemon juice and lentils.

SPRING GREENS
and Puy Lentils

50g Puy lentils
200g spring greens or
    curly kale, large stems
    removed, finely sliced
Drizzle of olive oil
1 garlic clove, crushed
Juice of ½ lemon

If not allergic

Serve with a little flaked fish such as salmon or mackerel.

1 Cook the Puy lentils according to the packet instructions (normally for about 25 minutes), drain and set aside.

2 While the lentils are cooking, bring a large pan of water to the boil, add the spring greens and cook for about 8 minutes, until the leaves are really tender.

3 Drain, reserving a few tablespoons of liquid for puréeing. Then plunge the leaves into some cold boiled water to cool down. Drain again, shaking off any excess water.

4 In a large frying pan heat the oil and add the garlic, then the Puy lentils, spring greens and lemon juice. Stir well and cook for a couple of minutes, until everything is heated through.

5 Purée, using some of the cooking liquid, to the desired consistency.

MAKES

3

PORTIONS

PREP: 5 MINUTES
COOK: 10 MINUTES

Swede is a delicious root vegetable that is easy to prepare and it is particularly tasty when combined with carrot. Quinoa is a great source of protein and will not mask the lovely sweet flavours of the carrot and swede but will add some protein to this purée.

QUINOA, CARROT
and Swede

20g quinoa flakes
200g carrots, peeled and chopped into small pieces
100g swede, peeled and chopped into small pieces

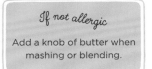

If not allergic

Add a knob of butter when mashing or blending.

1 Cook the quinoa flakes following the instructions on the packet, then drain and set aside.

2 Set a pan of water to boil over a high heat and place a steamer on top. Add the carrots and swede and steam for about 7 minutes, or until the vegetables are tender.

3 Then mash the carrot and swede with a fork or blend to a purée as desired and finally stir through the cooked quinoa flakes.

MAKES

6

PORTIONS

PREP: 5 MINUTES
COOK: 60 MINUTES

This purée is great for adding iron to your child's diet, and makes an uncomplicated introduction to meat. Iron from meat is easier to absorb that iron from other sources, and there is vitamin C in the sweet potato, which also facilitates iron absorption. Stewing beef normally takes a while to cook and become tender, but as we cut the meat into smaller pieces and purée it at the end, the cooking time does not need to be as long. If you don't wish to purée the meat you will need to increase the cooking time to 90 minutes to allow the meat to become very tender, so it will break up very easily.

SMOOTH BEEF
and Sweet Potato

1 tsp olive oil

200g stewing beef, cut
  into very small pieces

1 echalion shallot, roughly
  chopped

250g sweet potato, peeled
  and roughly chopped

400ml water

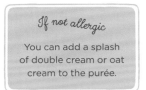

If not allergic

You can add a splash
of double cream or oat
cream to the purée.

1 Preheat the oven to 180°C/160°C Fan/350°F/Gas mark 4.

2 In an ovenproof pan, heat the oil over a medium to high heat, add the beef and allow it to brown. Then add the shallot and let it soften for a couple of minutes.

3 Add the sweet potato and the water, and bring to a gentle simmer. Cover and place in the oven for 1 hour, or until the meat is tender.

4 Remove from the oven and blend the ingredients together thoroughly until you reach a smooth consistency.

110 *Flavour Combinations*

PREP: 5 MINUTES
COOK: 15 MINUTES

Chicken thighs are tastier than chicken breast meat and they are also less expensive. In addition, dark chicken meat is also a richer source of iron for your baby than white chicken breasts. This is a delicious introduction to chicken casserole.

Chicken Thigh and
ROOT VEGETABLES

1 tsp olive oil
1 small skinless and
   boneless chicken
   thigh, chopped into
   small pieces
1 echalion shallot,
   finely chopped
100g carrot, peeled
   and chopped
100g parsnip, peeled
   and chopped
250ml water

1 Heat the oil in a saucepan over a medium heat and add the chicken, shallot, carrot and parsnip. Cook for 5 minutes over a medium heat, until the shallot is soft.

2 Add the water and bring to a gentle simmer, then cook for 10 minutes.

3 Check that the chicken is cooked and the vegetables are tender, then purée.

PREP: 10 MINUTES
COOK: 40 MINUTES

Chickpeas are a good source of plant-based carbohy-drate and protein so this makes a lovely purée for your baby to have for lunch or tea. You can also offer it alongside crudités or our Sweet Potato Wedges (see page 88) so your baby can dip them in. This is very fun (albeit messy) and the dipping action is good for practising fine motor skills. This purée will keep in the fridge in a sealed container for a day.

Red Pepper and
CHICKPEA

1 red pepper, seeds removed, roughly chopped
1 tbsp olive oil, plus extra for drizzling
1 garlic clove, skin on
400g tin chickpeas, drained and rinsed
Juice of ½ lemon

1 Preheat the oven to 220°C/200°C Fan/425°F/Gas mark 7.

2 Place the red pepper in a roasting tin with a drizzle of olive oil and place in the oven. After 20 minutes add the garlic clove to the roasting tin and cook for a further 15–20 minutes, until the pepper is nicely roasted.

3 Remove the skin from the garlic, then put it in a blender with the roasted red pepper, 1 tablespoon of olive oil, the chickpeas and lemon juice, and blend to a smooth paste.

If not allergic

Add a good teaspoon of tahini (sesame paste) when you blend all the ingredients.

EASY SNACK SUGGESTIONS

By now your baby may be hungry at different points in the day and might need a few additional small snacks to keep energy levels up. Whole fruit is a really easy option, but there are also plenty of ready-made ideas too. It is essential that you check labels for any allergens, and also it is worth taking note of the salt and sugar content of manufactured snacks, as brands vary.

- Whole fruit, sliced as appropriate.
- Gluten-free breadsticks – there are some great gluten-free brands, and some that are free from the top 14 allergens.
- Corn/Rice cakes – there are lots of brands aimed at babies and toddlers, with a variety of different flavours as well as plain ones.
- Gluten-free oatcakes.
- Dried fruit – pear, mango, pineapple or apple slices are all tasty and appealing. Make this an occasional snack, as dried fruit has a higher concentration of sugar than fresh fruit.
- Vegetable crudités such as cucumber and carrot sticks, with a choice of dips.

If your child is not allergic, you can also add:
- Hard-boiled eggs
- Cheese sticks
- Celery sticks
- Soft cereal bars (there are lots of brands designed for babies and toddlers)
- Small biscuits

5

Early Meals

Now that your baby has tried lots of different fruit and combinations of vegetables and meat from our First Flavours and Flavour Combinations sections, they should be ready to branch out further and experiment a bit more with Early Meals. These meals are based on well-known flavour combinations that have endured and remain popular, so they are a good next step on your baby's journey to joining the rest of the family at the table. While allergens are of course excluded, new herbs, spices and flavours are added, so these Early Meals will tempt your baby to become more adventurous and to try a broader range of tastes and textures. Because the meals generally include ingredients introduced in the Flavour Combinations section, these recipes will not be wholly unfamiliar and your child should be ready to really enjoy them.

It is nice at this stage to include more finger food and, as your baby is ready to become more involved with their food, you could consider offering them a spoon to hold at mealtimes to try self-feeding. We found that our babies loved this and were very pleased when they managed to actually scoop up a mouthful and pop it in. It was about playing and involvement and we still liked having our own spoons to speed things up a bit! At this point your baby should be happy eating a broad range of foods, including plenty of meat and vegetable options. Try to give your baby as much variety as possible. Remember you can always cook more than you need and freeze the rest for another time. As before, remember to keep mealtimes fun – if possible try to eat with your baby, or arrange play dates so your baby can eat with a friend and you can have some adult company.

At this point it's a good idea to offer babies a drink of water with their food from a beaker with a free-flowing spout (one that doesn't require babies to suck).

PREP: 5 MINUTES
COOK: 10 MINUTES

Pork and prunes are a classic combination. You can stir in some cooked rice or serve this with Sweet Potato Wedges (see page 88) and steamed vegetable finger food on the side to make a complete meal.

PORK
with Prunes

1 tsp olive oil
100g pork fillet, sliced
100g sweet potato,
   peeled and diced
100g prunes, stoned
150ml water

Label check
Check the prunes
for sulphites.

1 In a heavy-bottomed pan, heat the oil over a medium to high heat and then add the pork fillet.

2 Seal the outside of the pork then add the rest of the ingredients.

3 Bring to a simmer and cook for 7–10 minutes, until the pork is cooked through and the sweet potato is tender.

4 Chop up into small pieces or purée to the desired consistency, and serve.

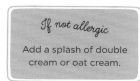

If not allergic

Add a splash of double
cream or oat cream.

MAKES

4

PORTIONS

PREP: 5 MINUTES
COOK: 25 MINUTES

This classic combination of carrot and coriander is made into a substantial meal by the addition of lentils, which are a source of protein and complex carbohydrates. We use ground coriander to provide the wonderful flavour, but you can use crushed coriander seeds if your baby is happy with the texture. We think this recipe is best served when half the quantity is puréed and added back into the mixture, giving a brightly-coloured stew full of texture. This goes well with gluten-free flatbread.

LENTIL, CARROT
and Coriander

1 tbsp olive oil

1 small echalion shallot, finely chopped

⅛ tsp ground coriander

200g carrot, peeled and diced

30g green lentils that do not require pre-soaking, rinsed

½ tsp finely chopped fresh coriander stem

600ml water

½ tsp finely chopped fresh coriander leaves

1 In a saucepan, heat the oil over a medium to high heat and add the shallot.

2 Cook the shallot for a few minutes until it softens, then add the ground coriander, and stir.

3 Add the carrots and let them cook for 2 minutes, then add the lentils, coriander stem and the water. Bring to the boil and cook for 5 minutes, then turn down the heat and simmer for 10–15 minutes, until the lentils are tender.

4 To serve, blend to the desired consistency and garnish with coriander leaves.

If not allergic

Serve with salmon.

You can also stir in some plain full-fat yoghurt or crème fraîche.

This is a very gentle nod to Indian cuisine. There is just a touch of aromatic spice but definitely no heat, providing delicious new flavours for your baby. You can mash or blend the diced butternut squash and carrot to whatever consistency suits your baby. We like to blend half and then add the other half back in to stir through to add some texture. It is lovely served with gluten-free flatbread or poppadoms to add some starchy carbohydrate and a variety of texture and you can also offer some steamed courgette slices on the side. This is great for adults too; just add some seasoning and some chilli flakes if you like a little heat, and the whole family can eat together.

MAKES

4

PORTIONS

PREP: 5 MINUTES
COOK: 50 MINUTES

Yellow Split Pea and
BUTTERNUT SQUASH DHAL

1 tbsp olive oil
1 echalion shallot, finely chopped
1 garlic clove, crushed
Pinch ground cumin
170g butternut squash, peeled and cut into small dice
125g carrot, peeled and cut into small dice
40g yellow split peas that do not require pre-soaking, rinsed
600ml water
Small handful, chopped fresh coriander, to garnish (optional)

1 In a saucepan, heat the oil over a medium to high heat and add the shallot. Cook the shallot for a few minutes until it softens, then add the garlic and ground cumin and stir.

2 Add the butternut squash and carrot and let them cook for a few minutes in the pan. Then add in the split peas and the water. Bring to the boil and cook for 10 minutes.

3 Turn down the heat and simmer for 30–35 minutes, until the lentils are tender.

4 Garnish with the finely chopped coriander leaves before serving, if using.

PREP: 5 MINUTES
COOK: 15 MINUTES

Chicken thigh is more flavoursome and adds a better texture to a purée than chicken breast, which can be a little drier. This is a lovely combination that has proved very popular with our baby testers. You can offer your baby some steamed broccoli florets on the side as finger food.

CHICKEN, SWEET POTATO
and Carrot

1 tsp olive oil
1 echalion shallot,
    finely chopped
1 large skinless and
    boneless chicken
    thigh, chopped into
    small pieces
150g carrot, peeled
    and chopped
100g sweet potato,
    peeled and chopped
200ml Simple Vegetable
    Stock (see page 180)
    or water

1 Heat the oil in a saucepan over a medium heat. Add the shallot and chicken, and cook for 2 minutes.

2 Add the carrot and sweet potato and let them sweat for a further 2 minutes.

3 Add the stock or water, bring to a gentle simmer and cook for 8 minutes.

4 Check the chicken is cooked, then purée the mixture.

If not allergic

Add a knob of butter when sweating the vegetables.

PREP: 2 MINUTES
COOK: 12 MINUTES

This rice goes very well with Early Meals such as Lamb with Mint and Aubergine (see page 134) and Mini Meals such as Chicken with Lemon, Garlic and Parsley (see page 172) and is very quick and easy to make. It is a little more interesting than plain rice, and introduces your baby to some new flavours that offer vitamin C and iron from the parsley and the spinach. You can add other herbs such as basil and chives if you would like some variation.

RICE WITH GREEN VEG

66g basmati rice
50g or 2 cubes frozen
   spinach
100g frozen peas
   (petits pois are best)
Small handful finely
   chopped parsley

If not allergic

Add in some finely
crushed tree nuts
or seeds for added
texture and nutrients.

1 Bring a pan of water to the boil and add the rice. Follow the cooking instructions on the packet.

2 In the last minute of cooking, add the spinach and peas, and wait until the water comes back to the boil before draining.

3 Stir in the chopped parsley, then serve.

PREP: 5 MINUTES
COOK: 40 MINUTES

This pesto is delicious, mild and creamy, and so good with gluten-free pasta. It has been a hit not just with our baby testers, but with bigger kids as well. As this makes enough for two portions, it is ideal for an easy teatime meal. You may find your handheld blender is too big for the job; we like to use the small attachment pot that comes with it. To make a more complete meal, serve it with a small piece of meat or fish (if your child is not allergic) cut into small pieces.

AUBERGINE PESTO
with Gluten-free Pasta Shapes

230g aubergine,
    roughly chopped
1 tbsp olive oil, plus an
    extra drizzle
Juice of ½ lemon
3 large basil leaves
120g gluten-free pasta

1 Preheat the oven to 220°C/200°C Fan/425°F/Gas mark 7.

2 Place the aubergine in a roasting tin with a drizzle of olive oil. Toss well ensuring that all the pieces are coated. Roast for 30–40 minutes, until it looks a little brown at the edges.

3 Put the roasted aubergine in a bowl with the rest of the ingredients apart from the pasta, and blend to a smooth consistency.

4 Meanwhile, put the gluten-free pasta in a pan of boiling water and cook, following the instructions on the packet.

5 Once the pasta is cooked, drain and put it back into the pan over a low heat. Stir in the aubergine pesto to warm it through.

If not allergic

Add a tablespoon of pine nuts to the pesto before blending. Although pine nuts are not tree nuts it is very rare to find a packet that does not have a 'may contain nuts' statement. Use ordinary pasta if your child is not allergic.

MAKES

3

PORTIONS

PREP: 5 MINUTES
COOK: ABOUT 10 MINUTES

This is a simple herb pesto that is great with spaghetti and pasta shapes. Do use ordinary pasta if your child is not allergic to gluten. Like other recipes that make a small quantity, you may find your handheld blender is too cumbersome unless you use the small pot attachment or you can increase the quantities if you prefer.

BASIL AND HERB PESTO
with Gluten-free Pasta Shapes

180g gluten-free pasta shapes
30g basil leaves
10g parsley, including stems
1½ tbsp olive oil
Juice of ½ lemon
Small garlic clove, peeled

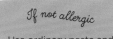

If not allergic

Use ordinary pasta and serve with grated cheese on top.

1 Put the gluten-free pasta in a pan of boiling water and cook, following the instructions on the packet.

2 Put all the other ingredients in a blender and blitz to a smooth consistency.

3 Once the pasta is cooked, drain and put it back into the pan over a low heat. Stir in the pesto to warm it through.

VARIATION
Serve the pesto on a plain piece of cooked meat or fish, such as plaice or lemon sole, if your baby is not allergic.

MAKES

4

PORTIONS

if puréed

PREP: 5 MINUTES
COOK: 60 MINUTES

This makes a nice side dish but it's also very good on its own. If you want to make a more substantial meal for your baby, serve with some cooked rice or cooked lentils.

Mediterranean VEGETABLES

2 echalion shallots,
    peeled and quartered
1 small aubergine, cut
    into bite-size chunks
1 small red pepper,
    deseeded and cut
    into bite-size chunks
1 medium courgette, cut
    into bite-size chunks
2 tbsp olive oil
150ml passata

1 Preheat the oven to 220°C/200°C Fan/425°F/Gas mark 7.

2 In a roasting tin toss the shallots, aubergine, pepper and courgette in the olive oil, and bake in the oven for 50 minutes.

3 Check the vegetables a few times during the cooking process. Once roasted, give the roasting tin a shake and add the passata. Return everything to the oven for a further 10 minutes.

4 Leave whole, mash or purée to the desired consistency.

If not allergic

Stir the vegetables
through cooked
cous cous.

PREP: 10 MINUTES
COOK: 20 MINUTES

These little patties are great for adding a little interest to mealtimes, and children love to pick them up. They are great on their own or alongside some of our other Early Meals such as Pork with Prunes (see page 119) or Chicken, Sweet Potato and Carrot (see page 122). If you make extra, freeze once pan-fried and then reheat from frozen in the oven as needed, ensuring they are cooked through.

POTATO, PEA
and Parsnip Cakes

300g floury potatoes
    such as Maris Pipers,
    peeled and chopped
140g parsnip, peeled
    and chopped
60g frozen peas
    (petits pois are best)
Drizzle of olive oil

If not allergic

Add a little cooked flaked fish such as cod or salmon into the mixture just before forming the patties, to make a fishcake.

1 Put the potato and parsnip in a saucepan, cover with water and cook for about 8 minutes, or until the potato feels soft.

2 3 minutes before the potato and parsnip are cooked, place the peas in a steamer above the pan and put a lid on top.

3 Drain the potato and parsnip, and mash with a potato masher to a smooth consistency. Stir in the cooked peas.

4 Allow the mash to cool a little so you can handle the mixture. With damp hands, so the mixture will not stick to you, form patties by rolling little balls and then pressing down slightly to make a disc shape.

5 Heat a little oil in a non-stick frying pan over a high heat, and drizzle in a little olive oil. Fry the patties for 3 minutes on each side, until golden brown. You may need to do this in batches, depending on the size of your frying pan.

Peter ran straight away to Mr. McGregor's garden, and squeezed under th he ate some lettuces and some French beans; and then he ate some radishes;

MAKES
5
PORTIONS

PREP: 5 MINUTES
COOK: 10 MINUTES

This is a delicious rich (but mild) dish and its creamy texture makes it very popular. You can serve this with a little rice if you'd like to add a bit more substance and texture. Chop the chicken as small as you need to, to suit your child.

CREAMY COCONUT CHICKEN
and Mango

Pinch turmeric
1 tsp ground cumin
Pinch ground ginger
½ tsp ground coriander
1 tbsp olive oil
2 skinless and boneless chicken thighs, chopped into small pieces
1 echalion shallot, finely chopped
1 fresh mango, peeled, stoned and chopped
400ml tin coconut milk

1 In a small bowl mix the turmeric, cumin, ginger and coriander together.

2 Heat the oil in a frying pan over a medium to high heat, then add the chicken. As it starts to take on a little colour, add the spices and shallot. Give it a good stir and cook for 2 more minutes.

3 Add the mango and coconut milk and bring to a gentle simmer. Simmer for about 5 minutes, until the chicken is cooked through and the coconut milk has reduced a little.

4 Serve as it is, or blend to the desired consistency. If you are blending, you may wish to reserve some of the sauce to ensure you get the right consistency.

Label check
Check the tin of coconut milk for sulphites and any added ingredients.

PREP: 5 MINUTES
COOK: 95 MINUTES

The lamb in this dish becomes beautifully tender and breaks up easily when prodded with a fork. This means it can be served without puréeing if your child is ready for more texture. Don't cut short the cooking time as the lamb needs a long, slow cook to make it easy to chew. Stir in cooked rice at the end if you'd like to add some carbohydrates and make a complete meal.

LAMB WITH MINT
and Aubergine

1 tbsp olive oil

150g lamb neck, chopped into chunks

1 echalion shallot, peeled and finely chopped

1 large courgette, chopped into chunks

1 aubergine, chopped into chunks

8 fresh mint leaves, roughly chopped

300ml passata

500ml water

1 Preheat the oven to 180°C/160°C Fan/350°F/Gas mark 4.

2 Heat the oil in a heavy-bottomed casserole dish over a medium to high heat, and add the lamb neck. Allow it to brown, then add the shallot and allow it to soften.

3 Add the courgette, aubergine, about a third of the chopped mint, passata and the water, and bring to a gentle simmer.

4 Pop on a lid and cook in the oven for 1½ hours, until the meat is nice and soft. If the lamb is not beautifully tender, put it back in the oven for a while longer.

5 Add the remaining mint leaves to the dish, and stir. Serve as it is, mash or purée to the desired consistency.

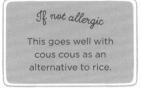

If not allergic

This goes well with cous cous as an alternative to rice.

PREP: 5 MINUTES
COOK: 95 MINUTES

Giving the meat a long, slow cook makes it deliciously tender and easy for little ones to chew. You can blend this if your baby is not ready to eat it as it is but you can also keep back a few pieces of tender meat for your baby to suck and chew on. This is a nice new texture to expose babies to.

BEEF, BUTTERNUT SQUASH
and Sweet Potato

1 tbsp olive oil

200g stewing beef, diced

1 echalion shallot,
   finely chopped

450g butternut squash,
   peeled and roughly
   chopped

80g sweet potato, peeled
   and roughly chopped

500ml water

Handful parsley (leaves and
   stems), finely chopped

1 Preheat the oven to 180°C/160°C Fan/350°F/Gas mark 4.

2 In a heavy-bottomed ovenproof dish, heat the olive oil and brown the diced beef. Once the beef has taken on some colour, add the shallot and allow it to soften.

3 Add the chopped squash and sweet potato, then add the water and the parsley and bring to a simmer. Pop on a lid and put the dish in the oven for 1½ hours, checking it every so often. Top up the liquid if necessary.

4 Make sure the meat is lovely and tender before serving – if not, pop it back into the oven for a while longer. Serve as it is, mash or purée to the desired consistency.

PREP: 5 MINUTES
COOK: 15 MINUTES

A velouté is simply a sauce made from stock and thickened by flour. Here we have used gluten-free flour. Ideally fresh stock should be used to give the best flavour. To make a more complete meal, you can add carbohydrates such as plain boiled rice or the fluffy centre of a jacket potato.

CHICKEN VELOUTÉ

1 tsp olive oil

1 echalion shallot, peeled and finely chopped

1 large skinless and boneless chicken thigh, chopped into small pieces

1 small garlic clove, peeled and crushed

3 large chestnut mushrooms, stalks removed and sliced

1 tbsp gluten-free plain flour

250ml White Chicken Stock (see page 181)

Small handful finely chopped curly parsley

1 In a saucepan, heat the olive oil over a medium to high heat, then add the shallot and chicken and stir for a minute or 2 until the shallot has softened. Add the garlic and cook for a further minute.

2 Add the mushrooms and flour and give everything a really good stir to combine. Add the stock, stirring continuously, bring to a simmer and cook for 10 minutes.

3 Serve as it is or mash or blend to the desired consistency.

4 Add the parsley at the end, just before serving.

VARIATION

You could use turkey instead of chicken.

If not allergic

Use butter instead of olive oil to give a richer sauce.

MAKES
6
PORTIONS

PREP: 10 MINUTES
COOK: 90 MINUTES

As the meat in this dish is so soft, you only need to purée it if you feel your baby can't yet manage this texture. If you are not puréeing, make sure the chickpeas are mashed with a fork so they do not present a choking hazard. This dish is full of new, mild flavours for your baby or toddler to try.

Easy
LAMB TAGINE

2 tbsp olive oil
2 medium carrots, peeled
    and roughly chopped
1 tsp ground coriander
1 tsp ground cumin
½ tsp ground cinnamon
¼ tsp ground ginger
1 garlic clove, peeled
    and finely chopped
1 small red onion, peeled
    and finely chopped
300g lamb neck, diced
250ml passata
100g tinned chickpeas,
    drained and rinsed
250ml water
2 handfuls spinach, washed

1 Preheat the oven to 180°C/160°C Fan/350°F/Gas mark 4.

2 Put 1 tablespoon of olive oil, half of the carrot, all the spices and the garlic and onion into a mini blender, and blitz.

3 In a heavy-bottomed ovenproof dish, heat the second tablespoon of olive oil and brown the diced lamb. Once the lamb has taken on some colour, add the spice mixture to the pan and allow it to coat the meat; cook for 3 minutes.

4 Add the passata, the rest of the chopped carrot, the chickpeas and the water to the pan and mix all the ingredients together. Bring to a simmer, pop on a lid and put it in the oven for 1 hour.

5 Remove from the oven and stir in the spinach. Return the dish to the oven for another 20 minutes.

6 Remove from the oven, cool and serve it as it is or mash or purée to the desired consistency before serving.

If not allergic

Serve with cous cous
if your child is not
allergic to gluten.

PREP: 5 MINUTES
COOK: 40 MINUTES

This is a tomato-based pasta sauce that is super with gluten-free pasta shapes or spaghetti, but is also lovely on its own as a purée, or with meat. We think it goes particularly well with our Meatballs with Quinoa – they are shown together on page 174. As it is so versatile, we recommend keeping a batch in your freezer for an easy way to make a range of meals more interesting.

Simple TOMATO PASTA SAUCE

1 tbsp olive oil
1 small red onion, peeled and chopped
1 large carrot, peeled and chopped
1 garlic clove, crushed
200ml passata
200ml water
1 tsp white wine vinegar
1 large bay leaf
Small handful fresh basil

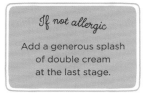

If not allergic

Add a generous splash of double cream at the last stage.

1 Heat the oil in a heavy-bottomed pan over a medium heat. Add the onion and allow to soften for a few minutes.

2 Add the carrot and garlic; give everything a good stir and allow it to cook for another minute.

3 Add the passata, water, vinegar and bay leaf and bring to a gentle simmer. Turn the heat down, cover and gently simmer for about 30 minutes.

4 Add the basil and cook for a further 5 minutes, then remove from the heat and remove the bay leaf.

5 Allow the mixture to cool before blending – either in a liquidiser or with a handheld blender – until smooth.

PREP: 5 MINUTES
COOK: 95 MINUTES

This is a lovely stew that contains plenty of root vegetables; it's warm and comforting and full of flavour. It goes perfectly with mash or a jacket potato. The meat is very tender and the vegetables are soft but you can purée this meal if that suits your baby's stage better.

CLASSIC BEEF
and Root Vegetable Casserole

1 tbsp olive oil

200g stewing beef, diced

1 echalion shallot, peeled and finely chopped

1 garlic clove, crushed

½ swede, peeled and chopped

1 small sweet potato, peeled and roughly chopped

½ medium turnip, peeled and roughly chopped

2 medium carrots, peeled and roughly chopped

500ml water

2 sprigs thyme

2 stems parsley, chopped

1 Preheat the oven to 180°C/160°C Fan/350°F/Gas mark 4.

2 In a heavy-bottomed ovenproof dish, heat the olive oil and brown the beef. Once the beef has taken on some colour, add the shallot and allow to soften for a few minutes, then add the garlic and the chopped vegetables and give everything a good stir.

3 Add the water, the thyme and the parsley, and bring to a simmer. Pop on a lid and put the dish in the oven for 1½ hours, until the beef is lovely and tender.

4 Remove from the oven and allow to cool before serving. You can mash or purée to the desired consistency, if you prefer.

MAKES

8

PORTIONS

PREP: 10 MINUTES
COOK: 15 MINUTES

In this recipe the chicken is poached gently in the stock with the other vegetables; it is very quick to prepare in one pot and the chicken is juicy and tender. You can serve with mashed potato or rice.

First
CHICKEN CASSEROLE

1 tsp olive oil
1 echalion shallot,
    peeled and sliced
1 garlic clove, peeled
    and crushed
3 small skinless and
    boneless chicken
    thighs, chopped into
    small pieces
200g sweet potato,
    peeled and chopped
100g chestnut mushrooms
    (or any cultivated
    mushrooms of your
    choice), sliced
400ml White Chicken
    Stock (see page 181)
Small handful parsley, finely
    chopped, to garnish

1 In a saucepan, heat the olive oil over a medium to high heat, then add the shallot and allow to soften.

2 Once the shallot has softened, add all the other ingredients and bring to a simmer. Cover with a lid and leave to simmer gently for 10–15 minutes.

3 Allow to cool, serve as it is, mash or purée to the desired consistency and garnish with parsley.

PREP: 10 MINUTES
COOK: 20 MINUTES

Potato and cauliflower is a classic and delicious combination. This has the addition of okra, which contains some calcium and adds an interesting new taste. As with all our recipes there is no heat in this, just gentle aromatic spicing to complement the vegetables. This is a nice teatime meal and also makes a tasty side dish to accompany other meals as your child gets older.

ALOO GOBI

150g new potatoes,
    peeled and diced small
150g cauliflower,
    broken into florets
½ tbsp olive oil
1 echalion shallot,
    peeled and sliced
½ tsp ground coriander
¼ tsp ground turmeric
⅛ tsp ground ginger
3 okra, trimmed and
    thinly sliced
100ml passata
100ml water
Small handful spinach,
    washed and shredded

1 Put the potatoes in a pan with plenty of cold water to cover. Bring to the boil and cook for 5 minutes, or until just tender.

2 Add the cauliflower to the pan and cook for a further 2 minutes, then drain the potatoes and cauliflower and set aside.

3 In a small frying pan, heat the oil over a medium to high heat, then add the shallot and cook for a few minutes to allow it to soften.

4 Add all the spices to the frying pan, then add the potatoes, cauliflower and okra and give everything a good stir. Add the passata and water and mix everything together, then bring to a gentle simmer and allow the sauce to reduce a little for 5 minutes.

5 Add the spinach and cook for another few minutes, until the spinach has wilted. Serve the dish as it is, or mash to the desired consistency.

If not allergic

Add some cubed paneer,
a delicious unsalted
Indian cheese.

PREP: 10 MINUTES
COOK: 10 MINUTES

This is not spicy at all, but creamy and full of gentle Thai flavours and aromas. Simply blitz up a paste to use as a base for this very quick meal. As this makes several portions, you can freeze most of it for future use. Serve with some plain boiled rice.

VEGETABLES
in Coconut Cream

For the paste

1 tbsp sunflower oil

Large handful fresh coriander leaves and stems, chopped

½ lemongrass stem, roughly chopped

1 large echalion shallot, peeled and roughly chopped

1 garlic clove, peeled

½ thumb-sized piece fresh ginger, peeled

400ml Simple Vegetable Stock (see page 180)

150g butternut squash, peeled and cut into small cubes

6 baby sweetcorn, cut into rounds

100g courgette, cut lengthways and sliced

60g broccoli, broken into bite-size pieces

160ml tin coconut cream

Handful frozen peas (petits pois are best)

1 In a small blender, blitz the paste ingredients to create a smooth paste.

2 Put the paste in a saucepan and cook over a medium heat for about 3 minutes, giving it a good stir now and again.

3 Add the stock and bring to a simmer, then add the squash, sweetcorn, courgette, broccoli and coconut cream and bring back to a gentle simmer for about 5 minutes, or until the vegetables are tender.

4 Add the frozen peas and cook for a further 30 seconds or so.

5 Allow to cool, serve like this or mash or blend to the desired consistency.

VARIATION

Add some cooked chicken and/or rice noodles for a more substantial meal.

Label check
Check your tin of coconut milk for sulphites and any added ingredients.

If not allergic
Add flakes of soft white fish like plaice or cod, or oily fish like salmon. Add small cubes of tofu if your child can eat soya.

MAKES

4

PORTIONS

PREP: 10 MINUTES
COOK: 25 MINUTES

This recipe uses paella rice, which is similar to risotto rice but easier to cook with. It does not need to be continually stirred, so you can get on with other things. Paella rice is widely available in supermarkets.

CHICKEN, RICE
and Peas

1 tsp olive oil
1 echalion shallot, peeled
  and roughly sliced
100g carrots, peeled and
  diced very small
1 garlic clove, crushed
150g paella rice
500ml White Chicken Stock
  (see page 181)
4 skinless and boneless
  chicken thighs, cut into
  very small pieces
100g cauliflower, broken
  into very small pieces
100g frozen peas
  (petits pois are best)

1 In a frying pan, heat the olive oil over a medium to high heat. Add the shallot and allow to soften for a few minutes.

2 Add the carrots and garlic and cook for a few minutes more, to soften.

3 Stir in the rice and coat it in the oil until it glistens, then add the stock and bring to a gentle simmer.

4 Add the chicken and cauliflower, and give everything a good stir, then leave to cook over a low to medium heat for 15 minutes.

5 Add the peas and cook for a further 5 minutes.

6 Check that the chicken is cooked through and that the rice is tender before serving.

If not allergic

Add a handful of grated cheese.

6

Mini Meals

Now that your baby is used to eating more complex foods with interesting flavours and textures, you can start introducing them to Mini Meals. This is a range of classic recipes, some of which have been adapted to appeal especially to babies and toddlers. The recipes provide a more complex range of textures and flavours that will help set your baby or toddler on an adventurous path of trying different things, safe in the knowledge that all the recipes are allergen free. Most of the recipes are suitable for freezing, which means you can cook a big batch that will provide quite a few meals. Mini Meals are not meant to be puréed, but you can mash them a little if your baby can't cope with the suggested texture. Meanwhile your toddler can try to eat these with a spoon; the textures make them generally easy to scoop up. This is also a good time to give your little one a baby fork to use to eat vegetables and meat. They have easy-grip handles and blunt, safe tines. Babies enjoy stabbing the food and trying to pick it up that way.

It is a great milestone when your baby can start eating the same food as the rest of the family and these recipes are the last stepping stone before they are ready to eat the same food as the rest of you. We have found that most of these recipes appeal to older children as well, and often the whole family, so you can start just cooking once for everyone rather than having to cater separately for your baby or toddler at every meal. Our children all loved these recipes and were very enthusiastic taste testers. It is tempting when you find a few meals that your baby particularly likes to keep serving the same selection over and over again. However, try to offer as much variety as possible; the wider range of different foods your child eats, the better. You can also

offer your baby things like fish fingers if they are not allergic – a very popular toddler meal – in our experience. There are several gluten-free options that are also free from other allergens, and they are nice served with oven chips. You can also buy pizza bases that are free from gluten, egg and other allergens, and you can add your own toppings according to your child's set of allergies.

This is the stage at which your toddler may start asserting themselves and may become a little fussy or difficult with food. We would suggest continuing to give your toddler a broad range of different foods. Have a look on page 48 for tips and advice for avoiding fussy eating. We know many babies who were very unfussy eaters but became picky as toddlers and that continued into childhood. Remember that if your child is suddenly refusing things it may well just be a short phase so don't get flustered and continue to serve lots of different meals. The most important thing, in our view, is to not get frustrated when your child refuses the meal you have taken the time to prepare. Try to remain calm and relaxed and remember that the odd skipped meal is not the end of the world. You may of course find that your toddler gives you no trouble whatsoever, moves seamlessly through the meals in this chapter and continues on the road of eating well and enjoying lots of different tastes and flavours.

We hope that once you have tried our selection of Mini Meals, your family will enjoy the recipes in our other book, *The Allergy-Free Family Cookbook*, which contains more than 100 different allergen-free recipes designed to appeal to the whole family so you can all eat the same meals regardless of food allergy.

These delicious little strips of chicken are perfect to dip into our Tomato and Vegetable Sauce (see page 177), and are even better when served with a side of Sweet Potato Wedges (see page 88). They are incredibly quick and easy, but do make sure the chicken is properly cooked but not overdone so you end up with succulent, soft pieces of chicken that little ones can easily eat. If you overdo it, you will end up with tough chicken that toddlers will find hard to manage.

Herby CHICKEN DIPPERS

1 small skinless and
  boneless chicken breast,
  sliced into thin strips
2 tbsp gluten-free
  plain flour
2 tsp olive oil
1 tsp lemon juice
1 small handful chives,
  finely chopped
1 small handful flat-leaf
  parsley, finely chopped

1 Dip the strips of chicken in the flour so they get a very light dusting, and pat off any excess.

2 In a bowl mix together the oil, lemon juice, chives and parsley.

3 Add the chicken strips and coat well in the oil mixture.

4 Heat a frying pan or griddle over a high heat and then add the chicken strips, cooking them for 2–3 minutes on each side, or until they are just cooked through.

If not allergic

Sprinkle over some sesame seeds and use ordinary wheat flour.

MAKES

4

PORTIONS

PREP: 5 MINUTES
COOK: 25 MINUTES

This is a simple risotto that is made with baby vegetables, perfect for little ones. It is a filling and comforting meal that is really easy to make and requires only one pan. This recipe uses lots of vegetables but it is easy to omit one vegetable and increase the quantity of another if you don't happen to have it. The rice offers an interesting texture but is very easy for a toddler to eat and your toddler should be able to manage this with a spoon (perhaps with a little help from you).

BABY-VEGETABLE *Risotto*

1 tbsp olive oil
1 echalion shallot, peeled
    and finely chopped
1 garlic clove, crushed
125g risotto rice
    (Carnaroli or Vialone
    Nano are best, as they
    give a much more creamy
    result than Arborio)
500ml Simple Vegetable
    Stock (see page 180)
2 baby leeks, chopped
2 baby courgettes,
    chopped
20 extra fine green beans,
    chopped
3 baby sweetcorns,
    chopped
4 stems thin asparagus,
    chopped, leaving tips
    intact and set aside
4 cherry tomatoes, halved
Small handful frozen peas
    (petits pois are best)

1 In a heavy-bottomed pan heat the oil, then add the shallot, cooking over a medium heat until soft, but not browned. This should take about 2 minutes.

2 Add the garlic and rice and keep stirring, making sure the rice does not stick to the bottom of the pan. When the rice starts to glisten, add a ladleful of stock.

3 Add the stock a ladleful at a time, waiting until is it almost absorbed before adding another one. Keep stirring and after about 5 minutes add the leek, courgette, beans, baby sweetcorn and asparagus, but not the tips.

4 Keep adding stock and stirring, and after another 10–12 minutes the rice should be tender. If at any time you need more liquid, just add more stock or water.

5 Stir in the cherry tomatoes, peas and asparagus tips and cook for a further minute. Remove from the heat and let the risotto rest in the pan for a few minutes before serving.

> *If not allergic*
>
> Add some grated Cheddar at the end of the cooking process or add some flaked cooked salmon when serving.

MAKES

4

PORTIONS

PREP: 10 MINUTES
COOK: 10-15 MINUTES

This is very nice served with rice or gluten-free pasta. When choosing your sweetcorn, remember to look for a version with no added salt or sugar. Kidney beans are a good source of protein and our kids love them.

Colourful VEGETABLE CHILLI

1 tsp olive oil

1 echalion shallot, peeled and finely chopped

40g red pepper, deseeded and sliced

80g carrot, peeled and chopped into chunks

50g tinned kidney beans, drained and rinsed

50g tinned sweetcorn, drained and rinsed

30g fine green beans, chopped

½ tsp ground coriander

1 tsp ground cumin

100ml passata

50ml water

1 Heat the oil in a pan over a medium heat. Add the shallot, pepper and carrot and allow to soften; this will take a couple of minutes.

2 Add the kidney beans, sweetcorn, fine green beans, coriander and cumin and give everything a good stir to combine.

3 Add the passata and water then bring to a simmer. Reduce the heat, cover and allow to simmer for about 10 minutes; the sauce will have reduced and the vegetables should be lovely and tender.

4 Mash a little to the desired consistency, and serve.

If not allergic

Serve with a little soured cream.

PREP: 15 MINUTES
COOK: 70 MINUTES

This is made with a 50/50 ratio of meat and mash, but you can easily adjust this if you prefer more or less potato. If you prefer you can use lamb mince instead of beef to make a shepherd's pie. We like serving this with some steamed vegetables such as broccoli or cauliflower on the side.

TRADITIONAL COTTAGE PIE

1 tsp olive oil
125g beef mince
1 echalion shallot, peeled and finely chopped
90g courgette, finely chopped
90g carrot, peeled and finely chopped
90g butternut squash, peeled and finely chopped
100ml passata
100ml water

For the topping
400g Maris Piper potatoes, peeled and chopped into small pieces
120g courgette, chopped into small pieces
Generous drizzle of olive oil

1 Preheat the oven to 180°C/160°C Fan/350°F/Gas mark 4.

2 Make the beef mince: In an ovenproof pan, heat the oil over a medium to high heat. Add the beef mince and allow it to brown, then add the shallot and cook until it just starts to soften.

3 Add the courgette, carrot, butternut squash, passata and water, and give everything a good stir. Bring to a gentle simmer, pop a lid on top and then place the pan in the oven.

4 Cook for 60 minutes, stirring occasionally.

5 Make the mashed potato: While the meat is cooking, pop the potatoes in a pan of cold water and bring to the boil. Cook for about 5 minutes until they are just starting to feel tender, and add the courgette. Cook for a further 5–10 minutes until the potato is soft, then drain, reserving a little of the liquid for mashing.

6 Mash the potato and courgette mixture, adding a good drizzle of olive oil.

7 Assemble the dish: Transfer the meat to individual ramekins or a suitable larger dish roughly 25 x 17cm and top with the mashed potato mixture. Pop the pies under the grill for a few minutes to colour the top slightly. Allow to cool a little before serving.

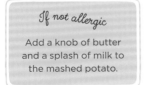

If not allergic

Add a knob of butter and a splash of milk to the mashed potato.

MAKES

4

PORTIONS

PREP: 10 MINUTES
COOK: 60 MINUTES

This is a delicious dish of layered chopped potato, vegetables and meat in a tomato sauce. There is no béchamel sauce as you would find in a traditional moussaka, but we don't think it needs it. We suggest that you make these in individual ramekins, or other small ovenproof dishes, as they are easier to layer up neatly and you can freeze any that you don't need. This is nice served with wilted spinach.

MINI MOUSSAKA

1 tsp olive oil
200g minced lamb
1 echalion shallot, peeled
  and finely chopped
1 small red pepper,
  deseeded and finely
  diced
1 garlic clove, peeled
  and crushed
1 tsp ground cinnamon
2 medium Maris Piper
  potatoes, peeled and
  finely diced
1 courgette, finely diced
1 medium aubergine,
  finely diced
4 fresh oregano leaves,
  finely chopped
300ml passata

1 Preheat the oven to 180°C/160°C Fan/350°F/Gas mark 4.

2 In a small frying pan, heat the oil over a medium to high heat. Add the lamb mince and allow it to brown. Try not to move it about in the pan too much to allow the meat to get a nice colour, which will give a better flavour to the dish.

3 Add the shallot and red pepper. Cook until they just start to soften, which will take a couple of minutes, then add the garlic and cinnamon and give everything a good stir.

4 Set out four 10cm ramekins on a baking sheet. Add a thin layer of the lamb to the bottom of each ramekin, then add layers of the chopped potato, courgette, aubergine and small sprinkles of the oregano. Keep layering up the ramekins until they are nearly full.

5 Add 75ml of passata to the top of each ramekin, then top with water until it nearly touches the rim of the ramekin. Lift the baking tray of ramekins into the oven, and let them cook for 45 minutes, or until the potatoes are soft and golden and the liquid has reduced to a thick sauce.

6 Cool the moussakas before serving.

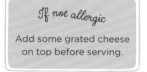

If not allergic

Add some grated cheese
on top before serving.

This is a classic dish that is universally loved and is great to introduce to your toddler. It isn't hot but full of gentle aromatic flavours, so it really appeals to younger children. If you think your child may wrinkle their nose at the idea of eating whole kidney beans and butter beans, these can easily be mashed up at the end of the cooking process to make a very smooth chilli. However, if you introduce them early your toddler shouldn't object, and they are a good source of protein and packed with nutrients. Our kids have always really loved them. Serve with a portion of long-grain rice and green vegetables.

MAKES

10

PORTIONS

PREP: 10 MINUTES
COOK: 65 MINUTES

Chilli CON CARNE

1 tsp olive oil

125g beef mince

1 echalion shallot, peeled
    and finely chopped

1 garlic clove, peeled
    and crushed

90g sweet potato, peeled
    and finely chopped

40g red pepper, deseeded
    and finely chopped

½ tbsp ground cumin

1 tsp ground coriander

100g tinned kidney beans,
    drained and rinsed

125g tinned butter beans,
    drained and rinsed

200ml passata

200ml water

1 Preheat the oven to 180°C/160°C Fan/350°F/Gas mark 4.

2 In an ovenproof pan, heat the oil over a medium to high heat, add the beef mince and allow it to brown, then add the shallot and cook until it just starts to soften.

3 Add the garlic, sweet potato, red pepper, cumin and coriander and give everything a good stir.

4 Add the kidney beans, butter beans, passata and water, and give everything another good stir. Bring to a gentle simmer, pop a lid on top and then place the pan in the oven.

5 Cook for 60 minutes, stirring occasionally. Cool before serving.

If not allergic

Serve with a dollop
of soured cream.

MAKES
9
PORTIONS

PREP: 10 MINUTES
COOK: 65 MINUTES

This is great served with gluten-free spaghetti or pasta shapes. Don't skimp on the cooking time – this dish needs an hour for the meat to become lovely and tender and to make a really rich tomato sauce. We often make a batch, feed the kids and instead of freezing the rest have it as an adult supper with the addition of a little seasoning.

SPAGHETTI BOLOGNESE

1 tsp olive oil
125g beef mince
1 echalion shallot, peeled and finely chopped
1 garlic clove, peeled and crushed
50g courgette, finely chopped
100g carrot, peeled and finely chopped
100g sweet potato, peeled and finely chopped
250ml passata
150ml water

1 Preheat the oven to 180°C/160°C Fan/350°F/Gas mark 4.

2 In an ovenproof pan, heat the oil over a medium to high heat. Add the beef mince and allow it to brown, then add the shallot and cook until it just starts to soften.

3 Add the garlic, courgette, carrot and sweet potato, and give everything a good stir.

4 Add the passata and water, and bring to a gently simmer. Pop the pan in the oven for 60 minutes, stirring occasionally. Cool before serving with the pasta of your choice.

If not allergic

Add a sprinkle of cheese on top when serving. You can use ordinary spaghetti.

PREP: 5 MINUTES
COOK: 25 MINUTES

Lemon and mint is such a fresh combination, and with the addition of chicken, this risotto makes a substantial meal for a toddler. This is an easy option for a baby or toddler to eat independently.

CHICKEN, LEMON
and Mint Risotto

1 tbsp olive oil

1 echalion shallot, peeled and finely chopped

½ skinless and boneless chicken breast or small skinless and boneless chicken thigh, chopped into small pieces

1 small garlic clove, peeled and crushed

125g risotto rice (Carnaroli or Vialone Nano are best, as they give a much more creamy result than Arborio)

500ml Simple Chicken Stock (see page 181)

60g courgette, grated

Zest of 1 lemon

1 tbsp lemon juice

4 mint leaves, finely sliced

1 In a heavy-bottomed pan heat the oil, then add the shallot and cook over a medium heat until soft, but not browned. This should take about 2 minutes.

2 Add the chicken and cook for a few minutes, until it is sealed.

3 Add the garlic and rice and keep stirring, making sure the rice does not stick to the bottom of the pan.

4 When the rice starts to glisten, add a ladleful of stock, then add the courgette and stir well.

5 Add the stock a ladleful at a time, waiting until it is almost absorbed before adding another one. Keep adding stock and stirring for about 15–18 minutes, until the rice is tender.

6 Remove from the heat and stir in the lemon zest, juice and mint leaves. Let the risotto rest in the pan for a few minutes before serving.

If not allergic

Instead of using chicken you can stir in some cooked prawns, if your child is old enough, at the end of the cooking stages.

PREP: 5 MINUTES
COOK: 25 MINUTES

This is a simple mushroom risotto using one type of mushroom – Portobellini, as we think they have a lovely flavour – but you can use any other cultivated (i.e. not wild) variety that you prefer or happen to have to hand.

MUSHROOM RISOTTO

1 tbsp olive oil

1 echalion shallot, peeled and finely chopped

2 garlic cloves, peeled and crushed

125g risotto rice (Carnaroli or Vialone Nano are best, as they give a much more creamy result than Arborio)

500ml White Chicken Stock (see page 181)

100g Portobellini mushrooms, sliced

25g Portobellini mushrooms, chopped into small pieces

Handful chopped flat-leaf parsley

1 In a heavy-bottomed pan heat the oil, then add the shallot and cook over a medium heat until soft, but not browned. This should take about 2 minutes.

2 Add the garlic and rice and then keep stirring, making sure the rice does not stick to the bottom of the pan.

3 When the rice starts to glisten, add a ladleful of stock, then add the mushrooms and stir well.

4 Add the stock a ladleful at a time, waiting until it is almost absorbed before adding another one. Keep adding stock and stirring for about 15–18 minutes, until the rice is tender.

5 Remove from the heat and stir in the parsley. Let the risotto rest in the pan for a few minutes before serving.

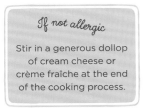

If not allergic

Stir in a generous dollop of cream cheese or crème fraîche at the end of the cooking process.

MAKES

8

PORTIONS

PREP: 10 MINUTES
COOK: 15 MINUTES

This is easy to make and a big hit with toddlers. There are lots of gluten-free brands of pasta, and indeed ordinary brands of pasta if your child is not allergic, that come in very small shapes ideal for babies and toddlers, and perfect for this recipe. This soup containing pasta and diced vegetables is another new texture for your baby to master and makes a lovely comforting meal.

MINESTRONE SOUP

For the base

1 tsp olive oil

1 echalion shallot, peeled
    and finely chopped

90g carrot, peeled and
    roughly chopped

1 garlic clove, peeled

3 cherry tomatoes

1 tsp olive oil

200ml passata

400ml water

100g very small gluten-free
    pasta shapes

75g courgette, finely diced

90g carrot, peeled and
    finely diced

Small handful chopped
    flat-leaf parsley

1 First make the base. In a small blender, blitz together the oil, shallot, carrot, garlic and cherry tomatoes.

2 In a large saucepan, heat the olive oil and add the base. Stir and cook for 2 minutes, then add the passata, water, pasta, courgette and carrot and bring to a simmer.

3 Cook for at least 10 minutes, and check that the pasta is tender. Add the parsley and give everything a good stir before serving.

VARIATION

This can be made heartier with the addition of some chopped cooked chicken.

If not allergic

Serve with a generous handful of grated cheese, and use ordinary small pasta shapes.

PREP: 5 MINUTES
COOK: 10 MINUTES

Most kids love Chinese cuisine, perhaps because of the sweetness, and this is a simple dish that is delicious served with a little portion of rice. It is extremely quick to rustle up, with ingredients we normally have in the fridge.

ORANGE
and Lemon Pork

½ tbsp cornflour

60ml fresh orange juice

20ml fresh lemon juice

50ml cold water

1 tbsp olive oil

3 spring onions, lower parts chopped and green tops discarded

50g pork fillet, sliced into thin strips

½ yellow pepper, deseeded and chopped

8 mangetout, sliced

4 baby sweetcorns, sliced in half lengthways

1 In a small bowl, measure out the cornflour and add the orange juice, lemon juice and water, stirring to combine, then set aside until step 3.

2 In a frying pan or wok, heat the oil over a high heat and then add the spring onions and pork and give everything a good stir. Add the yellow pepper, mangetout and baby sweetcorns, and keep everything moving around the pan or wok.

3 After a few more minutes – when the chicken is just cooked through – add the cornflour and juice mixture. It will bubble and thicken very quickly and create a thick sauce.

4 Remove from the heat when the sauce nicely coats the pork and vegetables, then serve.

This is not a complete meal, but rather a very nice accompaniment for some of our other meals, such as Herby Chicken Dippers (see page 152), or it goes well with a plain piece of grilled chicken or fish (if your child is not allergic). It is also a great way to use up any leftover new potatoes from a different meal. Jersey Royals are particularly good. Adding the optional olives gives a lovely flavour, and it is surprising how many toddlers love them. You can also mix through any herbs you have to hand in your kitchen such as chives, parsley or dill.

MAKES

2

PORTIONS

PREP: 5 MINUTES
COOK: 10 MINUTES

Crushed NEW POTATOES

200g new potatoes,
    scrubbed
1 tbsp olive oil
Handful green or black
    olives, pitted and
    chopped (optional)

Label check
Check the olives
for any added
ingredients.

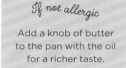

If not allergic
Add a knob of butter
to the pan with the oil
for a richer taste.

1 Put the new potatoes in a saucepan of cold water and bring to the boil. Once the water has boiled it should take about 8 minutes for the potatoes to be tender, but do give them a prod with a fork or knife to check.

2 Drain, and allow them to sit in the colander for a few moments for the steam to escape.

3 Heat the oil in a frying pan over a medium to high heat, then add the new potatoes. Using the back of a fork or a potato masher, gently crush the potatoes and toss them about in the olive oil in the pan. Mix in the olives, if using, then serve.

VARIATION

Instead of olives you can add in chopped spring onions or chopped chives.

This is a wholesome, warming winter casserole. A simple one-pot dish, it doesn't require any accompaniment so it is easy to serve and works well as a freezer-filler. While the Chantenay carrots are left whole in this recipe, and the lamb and potatoes are cut into quite big chunks so they don't disintegrate in the cooking process, you can always cut them smaller or mash the potato and carrots a little once the casserole is cooked if they are a bit tricky to handle. If your baby can manage it, this can be eaten with a baby fork, so your little one can attempt to spear the carrots and meat.

MAKES

6

PORTIONS

PREP: 10 MINUTES
COOK: 70 MINUTES

IRISH STEW

1 tsp olive oil

300g diced lamb shoulder or neck

1 echalion shallot, peeled and finely chopped

4 medium Maris Piper potatoes, peeled and chopped into chunks

1 large sweet potato, peeled and chopped into chunks

10 whole Chantenay carrots, or 100g ordinary carrots, peeled and chopped into chunks

1 leek, chopped into chunks

1 litre White Chicken Stock (see page 181)

2–3 sprigs thyme

1 Preheat the oven to 180°C/160°C Fan/350°F/Gas mark 4.

2 In an ovenproof pan, heat the oil over a medium to high heat. Add the lamb and allow it to brown, then add the shallot and allow to soften for a couple of minutes.

3 Next add the potatoes, sweet potato, carrots and leek, and mix everything together.

4 Add the stock and bring to a gentle simmer, then add the sprigs of thyme and pop the pan in the oven with a tight-fitting lid. Cook for 60 minutes, and check the meat is soft and tender when you remove it from the oven. If it does not break up when pushed with a fork, give it another 15 minutes' cooking time, until it is beautifully tender.

5 Remove the sprigs of thyme before serving.

MAKES
4
PORTIONS

PREP: 10 MINUTES
COOK: 5 MINUTES

This is a light and fresh dish, great served with some oven chips or Crushed New Potatoes (see page 170) and a side of broccoli and garden peas.

CHICKEN WITH LEMON,
Garlic and Parsley

1 tsp olive oil, plus extra for frying
Juice of 1 lemon
1 garlic clove, peeled and crushed
Small handful parsley, roughly chopped
1 skinless chicken breast, cut into strips

1 Mix the olive oil, lemon juice, garlic and parsley in a bowl, and combine well.

2 Toss in the chicken and leave to marinate for 5 minutes.

3 In a small frying pan, heat the oil over a medium heat and then add the chicken strips and any remaining marinade. Fry for about 2–3 minutes on each side, until the chicken is cooked through.

If not allergic

Use pieces of cubed salmon fillet, instead of chicken.

PREP: 10 MINUTES
COOK: 10 MINUTES

Everyone loves meatballs, and these are popular with kids as the added quinoa and apple makes them really moist with a hint of sweetness. These are easy to make, and it's very handy to keep a supply in the freezer. They go very well with our Tomato and Vegetable Sauce (see page 177) or our Simple Tomato Pasta Sauce (see page 140) as shown in the photo here.

Meatballs
WITH QUINOA

80g minced pork
80g minced beef
1 small apple, finely grated
½ echalion shallot, peeled
   and very finely chopped
40g cooked quinoa
1 tsp fresh parsley leaves,
   finely chopped
Freshly ground black
   pepper (optional)
Drizzle of olive oil

1 Preheat the oven to 200°C/180°C Fan/400°F/Gas mark 6.

2 Combine all the ingredients, except the oil, really well in a bowl. With damp hands, form into small, equal-size meatballs of 35g, or smaller if you like. If you don't wet your hands with a little water first, you'll find the meat will stick.

3 Heat a little oil in an ovenproof frying pan over a high heat. Fry the meatballs for a couple of minutes until they take on some colour. Transfer the pan to the oven for a further 8 minutes, or until the meatballs are cooked through.

MAKES

4

PORTIONS

PREP: 5 MINUTES
COOK: 15 MINUTES

This is not spicy at all, but is lovely and creamy and full of Thai flavours and aromas. Simply blitz up a paste to use as a base for this very quick meal and freeze so you've got some for next time. Serve with some rice and a little squeeze of lime juice. You can add a small tin of coconut cream when you add the coconut milk if your child needs feeding up.

CHICKEN IN COCONUT MILK

For the paste
1 tbsp sunflower oil
Large handful fresh coriander
    leaves and stalks, chopped
1 lemongrass stem, roughly
    chopped
1 large echalion shallot, peeled
    and roughly chopped
1 garlic clove, peeled
1 thumb-size piece fresh
    ginger, peeled

2 small skinless and
    boneless chicken breasts,
    finely sliced
400ml tinned coconut milk
6 baby sweetcorns, cut
    into rounds
100g courgette, cut
    lengthways then sliced
60g broccoli, broken into
    bite-size pieces
40g frozen peas
    (petits pois are best)

1 In a small blender, blitz the paste ingredients to a smooth consistency.

2 Put the paste in a saucepan over a medium heat and cook for about 3 minutes, giving it a good stir. Add the chicken and cook for 2 more minutes.

3 Add the coconut milk and bring to a gentle simmer. Then add the vegetables, except the peas, and cook for about 5 minutes, or until the vegetables are tender and the chicken is cooked through.

4 Add the frozen peas and cook for a further 30 seconds or so.

Label check
Check your tin of coconut milk for sulphites and other allergens.

If not allergic
Use any fish of your choice, such as salmon or cod, instead of chicken.

This is a delicious sauce that can go with a whole host of food, including gluten-free pasta or with a piece of grilled chicken or fish (if your child is not allergic). It is also good for children who may be going through a phase of rejecting vegetables as you cannot see any in the sauce once it is liquidised. If you prefer, chop the vegetables uniformly and then don't liquidise them at the end, giving you a chunky sauce that is just as delicious.

Tomato and VEGETABLE SAUCE

1 tbsp olive oil

1 small red onion, peeled and chopped

260g butternut squash, peeled and chopped

90g courgette, chopped

80g red pepper, deseeded and chopped

120g aubergine

400g tinned chopped tomatoes

200ml passata

200ml water

1 tsp white wine vinegar

1 bay leaf

1 Heat the oil over a medium heat in a heavy-bottomed pan, then add the onion and allow it to soften; this should take a few minutes.

2 Add the butternut squash, courgette, pepper and aubergine; give everything a good stir and cook for 1 minute.

3 Add the tinned tomatoes, passata, water, vinegar and bay leaf, then bring to a gentle simmer. Cover and pop the pan in the oven for 1 hour.

4 Allow to cool before blending until smooth, either in a liquidiser or with a handheld blender.

If not allergic

Stir in a little double cream or oat cream at the end.

PREP: 5 MINUTES
COOK: 10 MINUTES

This is such a quick and easy meal for a toddler – just serve with some boiled rice or rice noodles if you'd like to introduce a new texture. It is a fairly plain stir-fry with no sauce except for natural juices, which we find little ones really like.

Chicken STIR-FRY

1 tsp olive oil
1 spring onion, chopped
30g carrot, peeled and
    finely sliced
60g pak choi leaves,
    finely sliced
30g yellow pepper,
    deseeded and finely
    sliced
1 small skinless chicken
    breast, finely sliced
Pinch Chinese five-spice

1 Heat the oil over a high heat in a small frying pan, then add the spring onion, carrot, pak choi, pepper and chicken. Move everything about in the pan so it does not catch on the bottom and burn.

2 Add a pinch of Chinese five-spice, and continue to stir-fry for about 3–5 minutes, until the chicken is cooked through.

3 Add 2 tablespoons of water at the very end; it will mostly evaporate, but will help the nice flavours in the pan coat the chicken and vegetables.

VARIATION
Pork, turkey or beef all work well stir-fried.

Note
Check that your Chinese five-spice has no added ingredients such as sugar and salt. You just need: cinnamon, fennel, star anise, ginger and cloves.

If not allergic

Add some soya or Tamari (wheat-free) soya sauce.

PREP: 5 MINUTES
COOK: 35 MINUTES

You can make this ahead, cool and keep in the fridge for up to 1 week. If you like you can reduce it further to concentrate the stock and freeze, remembering to dilute again when using it in recipes. It is handy to freeze stock in clean silicone muffin trays placed inside a sealed plastic bag; you can then just use a few portions as and when you need them.

Simple VEGETABLE STOCK

1 tbsp olive oil
1 onion, chopped roughly with skin left on (this adds colour)
1 carrot, peeled and chopped roughly
2 garlic cloves, peeled and crushed
A few fresh parsley stems
4 black peppercorns
1 bay leaf
2 litres water

1 Heat the oil in a large heavy-based pan over a medium heat, then cook the onion and carrot for about 5 minutes, allowing them to soften.

2 Add the garlic, parsley, peppercorns, bay leaf and water, and bring to the boil. Reduce the heat and simmer very gently for about 30 minutes, skimming off any scum and fat as necessary.

3 Strain the liquid into a bowl, and discard the vegetables. Pour the stock back into the pan and reduce further as necessary.

If not allergic

Add a stick of celery, roughly chopped, to the stock.

This is easy to make after eating a roast chicken – be sure to keep the leftover bones. This stock is the basis for several of our recipes, and is easy to freeze. Simply reduce further to concentrate the stock and freeze, remembering to dilute again when using it in recipes. Like the vegetable stock, opposite, it's useful to freeze this in clean silicone muffin trays placed inside a sealed plastic bag, meaning you can use portions when you need them.

White CHICKEN STOCK

1 chicken carcass including any bones

1 onion, chopped roughly with skin left on

1 carrot, peeled and chopped roughly

A few fresh parsley stems

4 black peppercorns

1 bay leaf

2 litres water

If not allergic

Add a stick of celery, roughly chopped, to the stock.

1 Put all the ingredients in a large heavy-bottomed pan, then very slowly bring it to the boil.

2 As soon as the liquid boils, reduce the heat and simmer very gently for about 1 hour. It is the very low simmer that will give the best results and flavour – don't be tempted to boil it to speed up the cooking process, or you will end up with cloudy, fatty stock. Skim off any scum and fat as necessary.

3 Strain the liquid into a bowl, and discard the bones and vegetables.

4 Pour the stock back into the pan and reduce further, to about 500ml of liquid.

VARIATION

Roast the chicken and vegetables in the oven for about 60 minutes beforehand; this will give a brown chicken stock with a deeper flavour.

7

Puddings and Sweet Treats

WHOLE FRUIT IS A GREAT DESSERT OPTION

When you first start to wean your baby you will probably just give them a one-course main meal, but as they get older it is nice to introduce a dessert. Whole pieces of fruit are a great option as they contain fibre, vitamins and minerals and kids generally love eating them because they are naturally sweet. As well as whole pieces of fruit, we have given a range of fruit salad ideas. We find putting a selection of fruit together sometimes makes it more enticing and the children end up eating more than if we simply give them one whole piece of fruit.

You can also stir our fruit compôtes (see pages 66–69) through yoghurts or soya or coconut-based puddings, depending on your child's set of allergies. Our compôtes don't have any added sugar and dairy/soya/coconut yoghurts are sold in most supermarkets but do remember to check labels every time you buy, as ingredients and manufacturing processes can change. Also keep an eye on the sugar content, as many yoghurts and other desserts have high levels of added sugar. Fruit is the staple dessert for our children and has been since they were babies and fresh fruit is something they have every day.

We like to give them lots of different options and they love almost all fruit. We avoid kiwi fruit in our recipes as, although it isn't among the EU's most common allergens, it is nevertheless a relatively common one.

PUDDINGS AND TREATS

As well as giving your baby fruit as a dessert most days, it is also nice occasionally to give them a pudding or treat – perhaps our Apple and Blackberry Crumble at the weekend with the rest of the family or a Banana and Blueberry Muffin for breakfast one day.

We include recipes for biscuits and cakes in this book, as we think it is important to offer your toddler or older child a treat from time to time as part of an essentially healthy diet. When your child has allergies, you can't easily pop into a supermarket and buy these things. Most manufactured cakes and biscuits contain dairy, wheat and/or eggs and/or soya, and many may contain traces of nuts or other allergens that your child or baby may need to avoid. They often contain much higher levels of sugar than our desserts as well. Being able to make your own biscuits and cakes for special occasions is a must, and we've created some easy, fail-safe and most importantly, delicious treats that everyone can indulge in.

While you need to manage your child's sugar intake, we don't believe in restricting it completely as we think it may be counter-productive to completely avoid sugar. By turning sweet things into forbidden foods, you may actually be setting your child up for future problems and our view is that occasional treats play a part in an essentially healthy diet.

Most kids do have birthday cake and biscuits, and we think it is important to find a balance between limiting the amount of sugar your child has (particularly being aware of hidden sugars) without taking it off the table altogether.

PREP: 5 MINUTES
COOK: 2 MINUTES

Berries are universally loved by small children because of their sweetness and pretty colours and shapes. They are also packed full of vitamins. It is worth remembering that these fruits do have little seeds which offer another texture to introduce your baby to. Make sure you slice the strawberries, as they can be a choking hazard if left whole. This recipe is lovely with the addition of a small chopped fig.

BERRY FRUIT SALAD

6 strawberries, hulled
and quartered
6 raspberries
20 blueberries

Sauce ingredients
6 raspberries
½ pear, finely grated
1 tbsp water

1 Make the sauce first by adding all the sauce ingredients to a pan and heating over a medium to low heat for 1–2 minutes. Use the back of a wooden spoon to mash up the raspberries and mix all the ingredients together well.

2 Remove from the heat and pass through a fine sieve; we find a tea strainer works very well. Use the back of a spoon to press out all of the juice, then discard the seeds and set the sauce aside to cool.

3 Arrange the fruit in two bowls and top with the sauce.

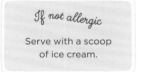

If not allergic

Serve with a scoop
of ice cream.

MAKES

4

PORTIONS

PREP: 5 MINUTES

100g melon, peeled and
chopped
100g pineapple, peeled
and chopped
60g mango, chopped
Small handful black
seedless grapes, sliced

Tropical FRUIT SALAD

We like to use Cantaloupe melon, with its vibrant orange
flesh, but Galia and Honeydew work just as well. You will
have leftover melon and pineapple, as they are large pieces
of fruit, so we suggest chopping the remainder and storing
it in the fridge for the rest of the family to eat.

1 Combine all the fruit, and serve.

MAKES

4

PORTIONS

PREP: 5 MINUTES

4 strawberries, hulled
and sliced
6 red seedless grapes,
sliced
6 white seedles grapes,
sliced
1 dessert apple, cored
and sliced
1 pear, sliced
Orange juice (optional) to
stop the fruit oxidising
and going brown

Classic FRUIT SALAD

This is a classic combination of fruit, and with the addition
of a little orange juice it will keep quite happily in the fridge
overnight; any leftovers can be eaten for breakfast the next
day. Please ensure you chop the strawberries and grapes,
as they can pose a choking hazard if left whole. If you
prefer, you can peel the apple and pear if your baby is
not yet ready to eat the skin.

1 Combine all the ingredients, and serve.

If not allergic

Serve with a splash
of single cream or
oat cream.

Many off-the-shelf sorbets and ice creams contain egg and dairy products as well as lots of added sugar. We urge you to try this recipe, as it takes seconds and creates a tasty and impressive pudding. It uses natural coconut water often found in the fruit juice aisle (this is not to be confused with coconut milk). Mango is the perfect fruit to use for sorbet as it does not contain any seeds and isn't tart like some berries. Most supermarkets sell bags of frozen mango, or you can chop and freeze your own. Any leftover sorbet can be frozen but will set very hard; you will need to remove it from the freezer to soften slightly before serving.

MAKES

4

PORTIONS

PREP: 5 MINUTES

Instant
MANGO SORBET

200ml coconut water
200g frozen mango,
 chopped

1 Put the coconut water and the mango into a bowl and blitz quickly with a handheld blender. They will instantly combine to form a smooth sorbet consistency, ready to eat.

MAKES

4

PORTIONS

PREP: 5 MINUTES
COOK: 30 MINUTES

This is a delicious traditional apple and blackberry crumble. We have included the option of adding in some ground flaxseed, widely available in supermarkets and health food shops and a great source of omega-3 – it also adds a nice crunch.

Apple and BLACKBERRY CRUMBLE

300g cooking apples, peeled and cored and cut into small pieces
1½ tbsp fresh orange juice
50g blackberries, cut in half if large
80g gluten-free plain flour
50g dairy-free sunflower spread
25g caster sugar
1 tbsp ground flaxseed (optional)

1 Preheat the oven to 200°C/180°C Fan/400°F/Gas mark 6.

2 Place the apple and orange juice in a saucepan over a medium heat. Allow the apple to break down a little and soften, then mix in the blackberries.

3 Fill 4 ramekins three-quarters full with the softened apples and blackberries.

4 Using a mini food processor, pulse together the flour and sunflower spread until they resemble breadcrumbs. Then stir in the sugar, and ground flaxseed, if using.

5 Spoon the crumble topping over the fruit, and bake in the oven for 10 minutes. Allow to cool before serving.

VARIATION

Use 350g chopped rhubarb instead of the apple and blackberries.

If not allergic

Serve with a scoop of ice cream. In addition you can use butter and/or ordinary flour in the topping. You can also add a tablespoon of ground nuts at step 4.

**PREP: 15 MINUTES,
PLUS CHILLING**

Most kids love jelly and it is so easy to make your own. Supermarkets sell little packets of leaf gelatine, measuring about 7 x 11cm, which are really simple to work with. You can set the jelly straight into small bowls, or if you want to create a centrepiece, use a jelly mould but you may well need to increase the quantities to fill it as we have done in this photo.

FRESH FRUIT
and Just Juice Jelly

4 leaves of gelatine
320ml orange juice,
    without bits
300g tinned mandarin
    slices, drained

1 Put the gelatine leaves in a bowl of cold water for about 4 minutes until soft. Remove the gelatine and shake off any excess water.

2 Place the gelatine in a small saucepan and set over a low heat for a few seconds, until it has melted. Pour the orange juice into the pan.

3 Stir until all is mixed well, then pour into individual bowls. Add the mandarin pieces and then pop the jelly in the fridge to set for at least 2 hours.

VARIATION
Any clear juice works well for jelly – we particularly like cranberry juice.

PREP: 5 MINUTES
COOK: 90 MINUTES

This is a classic, comforting dish that is really appealing to toddlers. Because this recipe uses natural coconut water, it has a subtle taste of coconut. Natural coconut water is not to be confused with coconut milk from a tin or carton. If you like you can add some fruit compôte (see pages 66–69) when serving.

RICE PUDDING

20g short-grained
    pudding rice
200ml coconut water
1 tsp caster sugar
Pinch grated nutmeg
    (optional)

1 Preheat the oven to 150°C/130°C Fan/300°F/Gas mark 2.

2 Rinse the rice in a sieve under running water, then place it in a small ovenproof dish.

3 Add the coconut water and sugar and stir. Sprinkle a little nutmeg on top, if using.

4 Put the pudding in the oven and leave to cook gently for 1¼–1½ hours, just until the pudding wobbles very lightly when shaken. Remove from the oven and allow to cool before serving.

If not allergic

Use ordinary milk instead of coconut water.

PREP: 5 MINUTES
COOK: 5 MINUTES,
PLUS CHILLING OVERNIGHT

Panna cotta might sound like a rather extravagant dessert for a baby but it is very simple, and babies love the smooth taste of the set coconut milk (and this is a good source of calories if your baby needs feeding up). Supermarkets sell little packets of leaf gelatine, measuring about 7 x 11cm, which are really simple to work with. It is quick to make but you will need to leave it in the fridge for a few hours – ideally overnight – to set.

Vanilla Coconut
PANNA COTTA

2 leaves of gelatine
200ml tinned coconut milk
1½ tsp vanilla essence
1 tsp caster sugar

Label check
Check your tin of coconut milk for sulphites and other allergens.

1 Put the gelatine leaves in a bowl of cold water to soak for a few minutes until soft, then squeeze out any excess water.

2 Put the coconut milk, vanilla and sugar into a saucepan and gently heat, then add the leaves of gelatine.

3 When the gelatine has melted into the coconut mixture – this will take seconds, take the pan off the heat and pour into ramekins. Place in the fridge to set.

4 Once set you can either eat it straight from the ramekin or turn it out onto a plate if you prefer.

If not allergic

You can use a 50:50 mix of double cream and milk instead of the coconut milk.

ICE LOLLIES

Ice lollies are so refreshing in the summer and are the perfect alternative to ice cream for those with a dairy allergy. These lollies are best consumed within 1 week. A key point to note is that cold reduces the perception of sweetness, so make sure your fruit is really ripe to give your lollies lots of flavour. However, if you wish you can add a teaspoon of soft brown sugar to any of these recipes.

Apple, Grape and Coconut

300ml fresh apple juice
20 seedless red grapes
120ml coconut cream
   (not coconut milk)

1 Blend all the ingredients together using a handheld blender, and fill your tray of lolly moulds.

2 Pop them in the freezer until set.

Label check
Check your coconut cream for sulphites and any other allergens.

Banana and Pineapple

2 overripe bananas
4 rings of pineapple from
   a small tin, including a
   little of the juice to taste

1 Blend all the ingredients together using a handheld blender, and fill your tray of lolly moulds.

2 Pop them in the freezer until set.

MAKES

4

PORTIONS

**PREP: 5 MINUTES
COOK: 5 MINUTES,
PLUS CHILLING OVERNIGHT**

This is a set, creamy lemon dessert that is simple to make. It is beautifully smooth, and uses coconut milk as a base. Use leaf gelatine, measuring about 7 x 11cm – which is readily available in supermarkets and really simple to work with.

Set Lemon
POSSET

**2 leaves of gelatine
200ml tinned coconut milk
50ml fresh lemon juice
1 tsp fresh lime juice
1 tbsp soft brown sugar**

Label check
Check your tin of coconut milk for sulphites and any other allergens.

1 Put the gelatine leaves in a bowl of cold water to soak for a few minutes until it is soft. Then squeeze out any excess water.

2 Put the coconut milk, lemon juice, lime juice and sugar into a saucepan and gently heat, then add the leaves of gelatine to allow it to melt. This will take a few seconds.

3 Give it a good stir, take it off the heat and pour it into 4 ramekins. Place in the fridge to set overnight.

If not allergic

You can use a 50:50 mix of double cream and milk instead of the coconut milk.

This recipe uses gluten-free oats, which are harvested and processed away from other cereals containing gluten. However, if your toddler can have normal oats, do use them. The longer you cook these flapjacks, the crunchier they will get, so you can adjust the baking time to suit your toddler. This basic recipe is delicious and not too sweet but you can easily add any extra dried fruit such as raisins or apricots to the mix. If you like a bit more crunch you can also add some milled flaxseed, or crushed pumpkin seeds when your child is one.

MAKES

20

PREP: 5 MINUTES
COOK: 20 MINUTES

Apple
FLAPJACKS

125g dairy-free sunflower
   spread
125g golden syrup
75g dates, finely chopped
75g dessert apple such
   as Braeburn, grated
   excluding the core
250g gluten-free oats

Label check
Check the packet of
dates for sulphites.

1 Preheat the oven to 190°C/170°C Fan/375°F/Gas mark 5.

2 Put the sunflower spread, golden syrup, dates and apple in a saucepan and, over a medium heat, melt together.

3 Once melted, tip in the oats and combine everything really well.

4 Tip the mixture into a baking tray, about 25 x 17cm, and press down firmly along all the edges.

5 Bake for 20–25 minutes. As soon as you remove the flapjack from the oven – while it is still hot – use a knife to cut it into squares, then allow it to cool in the tin before turning out.

If not allergic

Add a tablespoon of
condensed milk to make
a really squidgy, sweet
flapjack. Sesame seeds
also make a nice addition.

These are crunchy biscuits that are easy to rustle up, and they have a delicious mild citrus flavour. You can use any cookie cutter you like, such as stars, hearts, Christmas trees or spooky shapes for Hallowe'en like ghosts and bats.

Lemon
BISCUITS

75g dairy-free sunflower
    spread
55g caster sugar
40g golden syrup
2 tbsp lemon juice
Zest of 1 unwaxed lemon
210g gluten-free self-
    raising flour
½ tsp baking powder
Pinch salt (optional)

Label check
Check that your sunflower spread is dairy-free.

If not allergic
Use butter and wheat flour.

1 Preheat the oven to 190°C/170°C fan/375°F/Gas mark 5.

2 In a saucepan, over a medium heat, melt together the sunflower spread, sugar, golden syrup and lemon juice.

3 In a bowl mix together the lemon zest, flour, baking powder and salt, if using, and tip this into the saucepan. Stir to bring together a ball of dough, remove from the heat and allow the mixture to cool. Then wrap in cling film and pop in the fridge for 10 minutes.

4 On a surface dusted with flour, roll out the biscuit dough to about 3mm thick

5 Using a 5cm fluted cutter, cut out little biscuits and transfer them carefully to a lined baking sheet. Roll out any remaining bits of dough and keep cutting until you have used it all up.

6 Bake the biscuits in the oven for 10 minutes. They should be a pale sandy colour, and will still be a little soft when you take them out. Let them cool and firm up on a wire rack before serving.

7 Store the biscuits in an airtight container.

This is an old favourite that is a good alternative to cupcakes at parties. It is also great fun to get the kids involved in making them, as they are so easy to do. They keep well in the fridge in a sealed container for up to three days, and they freeze well too. This is the only recipe in the book where we have used chocolate. Dark chocolate tends to be naturally dairy-free but sometimes contains soya or is made in a factory that handles nuts. You need to find a brand that suits your child's set of allergies and that you are comfortable using.

MAKES

12

PREP: 10 MINUTES, PLUS CHILLING

Chocolate
CRISPIE CAKES

100g dark chocolate (70% cocoa solids), broken into pieces
50g golden syrup
50g dairy-free sunflower spread
100g free-from cornflakes

Optional toppings
Mini marshmallows
Dairy-free chocolate buttons

Label check
Check your cereal, dairy-free spread and chocolate labels carefully for allergens.

1 Put the chocolate, golden syrup and sunflower spread in a microwave-safe bowl and heat for 10 seconds, then stir and repeat several times until the mixture is just melted and smooth.

2 Add the cereal, and gently stir until it is all coated in the melted chocolate mixture.

3 Spoon the mixture into cupcake cases set out in a muffin tin. You can add toppings such as marshmallows or dairy-free chocolate buttons if you like. Put the cakes in the fridge to set, ideally overnight.

If not allergic
Use butter instead of dairy-free spread.

Cooking with your children can help reduce any anxiety about food allergy, and this is a great recipe to get them involved. This biscuit recipe has a subtle ginger taste to appeal to younger palates, but you can add more spice if you wish. Our children particularly enjoy helping to decorate the biscuits.

GINGERBREAD MEN

75g dairy-free sunflower
   spread
55g soft dark sugar
40g golden syrup
190g gluten-free self-
   raising flour
2 tsp ground ginger
50g icing sugar, sifted
1½ tsp water

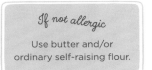

If not allergic

Use butter and/or
ordinary self-raising flour.

1 Preheat the oven to 190°C/170°C fan/375°F/Gas mark 5.

2 In a saucepan over a medium heat, gently melt together the sunflower spread, sugar and golden syrup.

3 In a bowl mix together the flour and ginger, and tip this mixture into the saucepan. Stir to bring together a ball of soft paste-like dough, then remove from the heat and allow it to cool a little. It will firm up and be easier to work with once it has cooled. You can wrap the dough in cling film and pop it in the fridge for 10 minutes.

4 Roll out the biscuit dough to about 4mm thick, directly onto your baking tray, lined with greaseproof paper. This makes it easy to peel away the excess dough, leaving your gingerbread men on the tray ready to bake.

5 Any remaining dough can be re-rolled to make more gingerbread men.

6 Bake in the oven for 8–10 minutes. The gingerbread men should look a little darker in colour, but will still be a little soft when you take them out. Let them cool and firm up on a wire rack before icing.

7 Mix the icing sugar and water to a thick consistency, and have fun decorating the gingerbread men. A piping bag will give very neat results, but most kids are happy drizzling the icing on with a teaspoon.

8 Leave the icing to set, then store the biscuits in an airtight container.

If you add the optional milled flaxseed to this recipe, it is an easy way to get some extra omega-3 into your child's diet. These are also really nice with a small handful of dairy-free chocolate chips instead of the blueberries. Whichever option you go for, they're delicious and a big hit with our children as well as all our toddler taste testers.

BANANA
and Blueberry Muffins

350g (about 3 large) overripe bananas, peeled and broken into rough pieces

60g soft brown sugar

55ml sunflower oil

1 tbsp fresh lemon juice

1 tsp cider vinegar

1 tbsp rice milk

210g gluten-free self-raising flour

1 tsp baking powder

¼ tsp bicarbonate of soda

¼ tsp xanthan gum

50g blueberries

25g milled flaxseed (optional)

1 Preheat the oven to 200°C/180°C fan/400°F/Gas mark 6.

2 Line a muffin tray with paper cases.

3 Using a stand mixer, or mixing by hand, combine the bananas with the sugar, sunflower oil, lemon juice, vinegar and rice milk in a bowl.

4 Thoroughly mix the flour, baking powder, bicarbonate of soda and xanthan gum in a separate bowl. Tip these dry ingredients into the banana mixture and mix well. Then stir in the blueberries and flaxseed, if using. Don't hang around – as soon as the mixture is combined, spoon it into the muffin cases.

5 Tap the muffin tin on your work surface to remove any large air bubbles, and bake on the middle shelf of the oven for about 20 minutes (test with a skewer or sharp knife – if it comes out clean without any raw mixture, it is cooked). Leave to cool in the tin for 5 minutes before turning out on to a wire rack to cool.

VARIATION
Replace the blueberries with 50g of suitable dairy-free choclate chips.

MAKES

12

PREP: 10 MINUTES
COOK: 15 MINUTES

This is a versatile sponge cake and works as a base for whatever kind of cake you'd like to make. Here we have used it to make little fairy cakes, perfect for little hands to pick up. Kids love to help with decorating and of course eating them. If you'd like to make a spectacular themed cake, you can use this recipe as a base and team it with our Easy Marshmallow Fondant Icing (see page 213).

FAIRY CAKES

150ml rice milk
30ml lemon juice
120g gluten-free self-
    raising flour
60g gluten-free plain flour
100g caster sugar
½ tsp bicarbonate of soda
½ tsp baking powder
50ml sunflower oil
20ml vanilla extract

For the icing
100g icing sugar, sifted
1 tbsp lemon juice
Sprinkles

Label check
Check the sprinkles
for allergens such
as gluten or milk.

If not allergic

Use soya milk for the
cake for a different,
slightly less airy, texture.

1 Preheat the oven to 220°C/200°C fan/425°F/Gas mark 7.

2 Line a muffin tin with paper cases.

3 Mix the rice milk and lemon juice together in a bowl and set aside. Don't worry if the mixture separates as it stands – you are making a buttermilk substitute that will help give the cakes a lovely light texture and activate the raising agents.

4 Mix the flours, sugar, bicarbonate of soda, baking powder together really well in a separate large bowl. Then pour the oil, vanilla extract and the rice milk and lemon mixture into these dry ingredients. Mix them together really well, either by hand or gently using a stand mixer. As soon as they are combined, pour the mixture into the paper cases.

5 Tap the muffin tin on the work surface to remove any large air bubbles and put it straight onto the middle shelf in the oven. Bake for about 15 minutes (test with a skewer or sharp knife – if it comes out clean without any raw mixture, the cakes are cooked).

6 Transfer the cakes to a wire rack to let them cool completely for at least 40 minutes. It's really important to let them cool completely before handling them. Once cool, the cakes are ready to decorate.

7 To make the icing, mix together the icing sugar and lemon juice a little at a time until you have a smooth consistency. Pour over the top of the cakes, then add your choice of sprinkles on top.

There are three elements you need to make a great celebration cake: the sponge base (see page 211), the filling and the icing over the top. Marshmallows are a well-known cheat when it comes to recreating a commercially manufactured icing. If you use pink marshmallows you will end up with pink icing, so there's no need to use extra food colouring. If you use white marshmallows, you can add any food colouring you like. We have used this recipe successfully to cover all manner of celebration cakes.

CELEBRATION CAKES
with Easy Marshmallow Fondant Icing

1. CELEBRATION CAKE BASE

To make two 20cm diameter sponge cakes, you will need a double quantity of Fairy Cake mixture (see page 211). To prepare your cake tins, simply wipe a little oil around the insides and then lightly dust with icing sugar. Divide the mixture equally between the two tins and bake in a preheated oven at 220°C/200°C fan/425°F/Gas mark 7 for 35–40 minutes.

2. BUTTER CREAM FILLING

150g dairy-free sunflower spread
100g icing sugar
Food colourings if required for your design, and flavourings, such as vanilla extract, to taste

This buttercream recipe will be enough to generously sandwich two 20cm layers of cake together. Use an electric whisk to combine the ingredients. If you like you can also add a layer of jam when sandwiching your cakes together.

3. MARSHMALLOW FONDANT ICING

PREP: 10 MINUTES
COOK: 5 MINUTES

150g white mini
   marshmallows
300g icing sugar
½–1 tsp water as needed
Food colouring as desired

1 Set a pan of water over a high heat and bring to the boil.

2 Set a heatproof bowl on top of the boiling water, and add the marshmallows. With an oven glove to protect your hand from the steam, use a silicone spatula or wooden spoon to stir occasionally, and allow the marshmallow to totally melt. This will take about 5 minutes. It will look like a sticky mess, but don't be alarmed – it is supposed to!

3 Make sure all the marshmallows are melted before you remove the bowl from the heat.

4a If using a stand mixer: With a paddle attachment on a low speed, start mixing, gradually adding the icing sugar. Once all the icing sugar is incorporated, gradually add the water until the icing forms a ball. There may be some mixture stuck on the sides of the bowl, scrape it off and keep mixing.

4b If mixing by hand: Add roughly half of the icing sugar to the marshmallow mix, dust your hands well with icing sugar and start to knead the marshmallows and icing sugar together – it will be really sticky to start with, but don't worry – it comes together quite quickly. Gradually add the water and the remaining icing sugar and continue kneading until it forms a ball of icing.

5 If you're using food colouring, knead it into the ball of icing as required.

6 It is now ready to roll out on a surface dusted with a little icing sugar. Use it to decorate your cake as you wish.

FIRST BIRTHDAY PARTY

A first birthday marks the end of an era, but also the start of an exciting new one. It's lovely to celebrate it with a traditional birthday party with all the trimmings, and there is no reason whatsoever that food allergy should make it any less special for your child or more stressful for you. Here we give you some tips for hosting your own party, including what to serve and how to manage the risk of cross-contamination, as well as tips for attending other parties.

HOSTING A PARTY

If you are serving food for adults as well as children, we would recommend serving allergy-free food to everyone. This way you don't have to worry about cross-contamination if food is dropped and picked up by your allergic baby, or if it is dropped into other bowls of food across the table. If you don't have a child with an allergy it's hard to remember to be cautious, so if all the food is safe for everyone, it makes things more straightforward.

Opposite is a list of suggestions that will work really well and recipes that you can make, including a lovely birthday cake that is perfect for any party and can be adapted to suit any theme you like. We don't think many will notice that there are no allergens in the food you are serving, because it is all normal party food that tastes delicious.

If you are hosting at home it is very easy to manage cross-contamination, but if you are in a venue such as a village hall it is harder, as you do not know what food has been prepared in the facilities beforehand. Take your own clean cloths to wipe down any surfaces, and as far as you can, prepare all food at home and then transport it to the venue. We find that pre-packing all the food into individual party boxes complete with a drink works very well.

If you are going to a venue such as a soft play centre where they are providing the food, speak to the manager well in advance and get a good understanding of whether they can cater for your specific requirements. It is always worth asking if they would be happy if you provided the food instead if they are not easily able to cater for you.

PARTY MENU

- Crudités – chop up sticks of vegetables; we find carrot and cucumber are universally popular with kids, and little cherry tomatoes cut in quarters are also good to have. In addition, sugarsnap peas, baby sweetcorn and asparagus are well recieved but you will need to cook them for a minute or so in boiling water and then plunge them into cold water to stop them cooking and help them keep their vibrant colour.
- Red Pepper and Chickpea dip (see page 114).
- Crisps – it wouldn't be a party without crisps, but remember to check labels carefully as some brands contain a range of allergens and many have a high salt

content. Go for a few different varieties, as all kids and adults love crisps.

- Sandwiches and wraps – use a suitable gluten-free bread or flatbread, and choose fillings such as ham and cucumber, or jam. You can use a cookie cutter to make the sandwiches into different shapes.
- Cocktail sausages – use a suitable allergen-free brand, and if you can't find cocktail-size sausages, use chipolatas and chop them into three before cooking. Serve plain or with ketchup.
- Allergen-free fish fingers and oven chips make an easy party treat if your child can have fish.
- Drinks – you can't go wrong with offering water and juice or squash. We find kids often like mini individual bottles of water.
- Fairy Cakes (see page 211).
- Birthday Cake (see page 212).
- Chocolate Crispie Cakes (see page 203).
- Sliced pieces of fruit – grapes and strawberries are always a big hit.
- Jelly (see page 192). If you make the jellies in little disposable pots you have the added bonus of no washing up.
- Ice cream – there are some really good allergen-free brands of ice cream available, often with a coconut base for dairy-free varieties – check labels carefully to find a suitable brand.
- Biscuits – always check labels very carefully, but there are lots of great allergen-free biscuits available in supermarkets designed for kids, or you can make our Lemon Biscuits (see page 202) or Gingerbread Men (see page 206).

ATTENDING A PARTY

You need to be careful when going to parties. Often the most well-meaning host can get it wrong if they don't understand food allergy. Our advice is simply to take along your own food for your child and make the host aware of your child's allergies. The parents will often be grateful that you are providing your own food so they don't need to worry about it. Just keep a keen eye on your child while food is about to ensure they don't pick up any food containing an allergen, and don't forget to keep any medications such as EpiPens, inhalers and antihistamines to hand.

FURTHER ADVICE

FOOD HYGIENE, FREEZING AND DEFROSTING

The advice below is not allergy specific, but you need to be extra careful about food hygiene with babies. Most hygiene guidelines are common sense, but are still worth noting. It's important to sterilise baby equipment – especially bottles – until babies are 12 months old.

KITCHEN HYGIENE

- Your fridge should run at 5°C or below.
- Your freezer should run at -18°C.
- Use separate chopping boards for raw meat and raw fish.
- Wash and replace kitchen cloths frequently, as they are an attractive place for bacteria to multiply.
- Don't leave out food that needs to be chilled, as bacteria multiply quickly at room temperature.

RAW MEAT AND FISH

Raw meat and fish can contain bacteria that cause food poisoning, such as Salmonella and E. coli. It is important to follow some basic rules when dealing with raw meat or fish.

- Wash hands before cooking and after handling any raw food.
- Store raw meat at the bottom of your fridge, covered and away from other foods.
- Don't wash raw meat – this will just spread any bacteria around your sink.
- When preparing raw meat keep other food out of the way, especially if it is not going to be cooked.
- Use a separate chopping board for raw meat.
- When meat is cooked properly any bacteria will be killed.
- Chicken should be cooked thoroughly and must never have any pink meat or bloody juices.
- Cooked pork should not be served rare or have any bloody juices, and should be particularly well cooked for babies.
- Beef can be served rare for adults provided the outside of the meat (where bacteria can lie) is seared, but should be well cooked throughout for babies and small children.

RAW FRUIT AND VEGETABLES

Always wash fruit and vegetables before eating to remove any dirt or germs that may be present on the surface. Peeling fruit and vegetables also does the same job, and you can peel items such as cucumbers and courgettes.

RICE

Rice is a food that you need to be careful with in terms of food safety. It can contain spores from a type of bacteria that can cause food poisoning. If rice is cooked properly, i.e. it is steaming hot, then you won't have any problems. If you leave your cooked rice out at room temperature the bacteria can start to multiply. Follow these basic rules:

- Always check rice is piping hot all the way through if serving hot.
- If using cold rice (for salads, for example) chill the rice down to room temperature quickly (ideally in less than 1 hour), and then put it in the fridge.
- Don't leave the rice in the pan to cool down; use a separate plate and spread the rice out so it cools more quickly.
- Fridge-cold rice is safe, as the bacteria cannot multiply.
- If you reheat rice that has been cooked previously, ensure it is piping hot before serving.

STORING LEFTOVER FOOD

- Cool any food to room temperature as quickly as you can, and then put it in the fridge or freezer.
- Don't leave food in the pan to cool down; use a shallow dish and spread it out, or put it into the smaller containers you plan to chill/freeze it in.
- Do not put hot or warm food in the fridge or freezer.
- If you have made too much and haven't served it to your baby, you can refrigerate it in a sealed container and offer it to your baby the following day, or freeze in portions.
- If your baby has eaten from a dish or tub and then hasn't finished, discard this food. You mustn't reuse it.

STORING FROZEN FOOD

If you use small tubs or ice-cube trays you will find freezing portions of baby food is very easy. One good technique is to freeze a sillicone muffin tray of food and, when frozen, tip the frozen cubes into a ziplock bag, and then you have the tray free for your next batch of food.

DEFROSTING FOOD PORTIONS

Food must be defrosted thoroughly before reheating. If you are organised, defrost food in the fridge overnight, but we prefer the convenience of a defrost setting on the microwave. It is not sufficient to simply warm the food through. Remember to make sure the food is piping hot throughout when reheating, and allow it to cool a little before serving. Any food that has been frozen and defrosted and reheated cannot then be reheated or refrozen, so discard any food not eaten.

STARTING NURSERY AND DAY CARE

Regardless of food allergy it can be daunting when you start thinking about leaving your baby in the charge of others, whether it's a nursery, childminder, nanny or even with grandparents. Food allergy complicates things and can make the experience more of a worry, but it doesn't need to be. Clear communication can calm a lot of anxiety, and asking the right questions and getting straight answers that give you confidence can make all the difference. We have been very lucky that our children's nurseries (and later schools) have been exemplary in how they have managed our children's food allergies, and they were able to answer all our questions to reassure us. However, when looking around day care and nursery settings we felt some took allergy a lot more seriously than others – so when you're looking for a nursery, nanny or childminder it can be helpful to be prepared and ask the right questions. With nannies and childminders things are more straightforward, as you can be more prescriptive about how you'd like things done, but with nurseries there are more children to consider, so think through the things you'd like to know more about when you're looking around and when your baby or toddler starts.

We also feel it's important for you as a parent to offer suggestions in coming up with a plan if you're not completely happy with the one that's in place. Equally, you can do a lot to ensure your child is included in activities. We both brought in recipes for free-from cakes and biscuits when the nursery was doing baking activities, and provided alternative options for Easter egg hunts. We didn't expect the nurseries to think of everything, but generally they were exceptionally accommodating – we are very grateful for that – and we don't feel our children missed out on anything.

It's important that a nursery understands the severity of your baby's allergy, so don't just assume people are aware of the seriousness of food allergy or your child's particular circumstances. Bring your doctor's emergency treatment plan to the nursery, outlining under what circumstances different medication should be used and when an ambulance should be called.

Ask lots of questions when you visit a nursery so you get a sense of how staff will deal with your baby's allergy and their attitude towards allergy. Questions you may like to ask include the following:

- Does the nursery have a protocol or strategy for dealing with food allergy?
- Do they have experience of dealing with other food-allergic babies and children?
- Where will medication be kept?
- Are all members of staff trained to use an adrenaline auto-injector?
- Will the nursery cater for your child's allergy, or will you need to bring in food?
- If the nursery is providing food, is it prepared on or off site, and can you talk to the catering staff?
- How will the risk of cross-contamination with other small children consuming allergens (often messily) be managed?
- Can you bring in recipes and bake cakes or other treats your child can have?

There's absolutely no reason your baby or toddler shouldn't get just as much fun and pleasure out of nursery as everyone else.

MENU PLANNERS

EXAMPLE MENU PLANNER <u>AFTER</u> THE FIRST MONTH OF WEANING

	BREAKFAST	MID-MORNING	LUNCH
MONDAY	Gluten-free toast soldiers		Red Pepper and Butternut Squash Serve with: Steamed broccoli Dessert: Apple Sauce
TUESDAY	Mashed banana		Carrot and Coriander Serve with: Steamed asparagus spears Dessert: Sliced strawberries
WEDNESDAY	Apple Sauce		Smooth Beef and Sweet Potato Serve with: Steamed carrot batons Dessert: Apricot Compôte
THURSDAY	Free-from porridge with usual milk		Red Pepper and Chickpea Serve with: Steamed fine green beans Dessert: Sliced melon
FRIDAY	Apricot Compôte		Quinoa, Carrot and Swede Serve with: Steamed cauliflower florets Dessert: Sliced papaya
SATURDAY	Soft melon slices		Butter Bean and Butternut Squash Serve with: Steamed broccoli florets Dessert: Instant Mango Sorbet
SUNDAY	Gluten-free toast soldiers		Chicken Thigh and Root Vegetables Serve with: Steamed carrot batons Dessert: Sliced grapes and raspberries

MID-AFTERNOON	TEA
	Sweet Potato and Cabbage
	Cavolo Nero with Butternut Squash
	Peas, Spinach and New Potatoes
	Parsnip and Butternut Squash
	Pea and Mint
	Lentil, Carrot and Coriander
	Courgette and Aubergine

Depending on when your baby started weaning they could be anywhere between five and seven months old. Your baby will be really used to lots of different vegetables and fruit by now, and will have moved on to more protein-dense foods. You can also introduce some snacks if you feel your baby needs them. This menu planner offers suggestions, and you can adapt them to fit in with your routine. If you'd like to, you can serve lunch with some extra carbohydrates such as rice and potatoes.

EXAMPLE MENU PLANNER FOR 9–12 MONTHS

	BREAKFAST	MID-MORNING	LUNCH
MONDAY	Apple Sauce	Rice cakes	First Chicken Casserole Dessert: Fresh mango
TUESDAY	Mashed banana	Cucumber sticks	Lamb with Mint and Aubergine Dessert: Sliced pear
WEDNESDAY	Gluten-free toast soldiers	Melon slices	Creamy Coconut Chicken and Mango Serve with: Plain rice and veg Dessert: Fresh sliced pineapple
THURSDAY	Apricot Compôte	Sliced grapes	Minestrone Soup Dessert: Blueberries
FRIDAY	Black Forest Compôte	Banana	Chicken Velouté Serve with: Plain rice and veg Dessert: Raspberries
SATURDAY	Gluten-free toast soldiers	Sliced strawberries	Pork with Prunes Serve with: Sweet Potato Wedges and greens Dessert: Rice Pudding
SUNDAY	Gluten-free porridge with usual milk	Sliced peach	Lamb Tagine Serve with: Rice Dessert: Instant Mango Sorbet

MID-AFTERNOON	TEA
...aisins	Lentil, Carrot and Coriander
...ple slices	Potato, Pea and Parsnip Cakes
...ngerine	Yellow Split Pea and Butternut Squash Dhal
...uten-free breadsticks	Chicken, Sweet Potato and Carrot
...ucumber sticks	Aubergine Pesto with Gluten-free Pasta Shapes
...gmented orange	Mediterranean Vegetables
...ce cakes	Aloo Gobi

By the time your baby is nine months old you will really be feeling in the swing of things. They will be eating a wide range of food and textures, and having three meals a day with the addition of snacks to help keep their energy levels up.

EXAMPLE MENU PLANNER FOR 12–18 MONTHS

	BREAKFAST	MID-MORNING	LUNCH
MONDAY	Gluten-free porridge with usual milk	Sliced grapes	Mushroom Risotto Serve with: Steamed fine green beans Dessert: Sliced apple and strawberries
TUESDAY	Banana and dairy-free yoghurt	Raisins and cucumber sticks	Lamb with Mint and Aubergine Serve with: Rice and steamed cur kale Dessert: Sliced nectarine
WEDNESDAY	Gluten-free toast soldiers	Sliced peach	Spaghetti Bolognese Serve with: Sliced cherry tomato Dessert: Raspberries
THURSDAY	Gluten-free porridge with usual milk	Gluten-free breadsticks	Herby Chicken Dippers Serve with: Crushed New Potato Tomato and Vegetable Sauce Dessert: Berry Fruit Salad
FRIDAY	Gluten-free cereal with usual milk	Rice cakes	Mini Moussaka Serve with: Peas Dessert: Stone Fruit Compôte
SATURDAY	Gluten-free toast soldiers	Orange segments	Cottage Pie Serve with: Peas Dessert: Apple and Blackberry Crumble
SUNDAY	Banana and Blueberry Muffin	Blueberries	Roast chicken (with rest of family Dessert: Rice Pudding with Apric Compôte

MID-AFTERNOON	TEA
ce cakes	First Chicken Casserole Serve with: Steamed broccoli florets Dessert: Segmented orange
rawberries	Chicken, Rice and Peas Dessert: Tropical Fruit Salad
ucumber, red pepper d carrot sticks	Vegetables in Coconut Cream Serve with: Rice with Green Veg Dessert: Blueberries and strawberries
ced melon	Yellow Split Pea and Butternut Squash Dhal Serve with: Poppadum Dessert: Banana
mon Biscuit	Basil and Herb Pesto with Gluten-free Pasta Shapes Serve with: Shredded baby gem lettuce Dessert: Chopped pineapple
ngerbread Man	Chilli con Carne Dessert: Fresh Fruit and Just Juice Jelly
ple Flapjack	Chicken Stir-fry Serve with: Plain boiled rice Dessert: Ice Lolly

Now your baby has reached their first birthday they should be growing fast and eating well. They will be having three good meals a day, with dessert at lunch and teatime as well as additional snacks throughout the day.

EXAMPLE MENU PLANNER FOR 18 MONTHS ONWARDS

	BREAKFAST	MID-MORNING	LUNCH
MONDAY	Gluten-free porridge with usual milk and Stone Fruit Compôte	Banana and rice cakes	Baby Vegetable Risotto Dessert: Segmented orange
TUESDAY	Gluten-free cereal with usual milk	Apple slices	Irish Stew Serve with: Steamed fine green beans Dessert: Coconut yoghurt
WEDNESDAY	Gluten-free toast with dairy-free spread	Watermelon	Spaghetti Bolognese Serve with: Steamed broccoli Pudding: Fresh Fruit and Just Juice Jelly
THURSDAY	Tropical Fruit Salad and gluten-free toast	Cucumber sticks and Red Pepper and Chickpea dip	Mini Moussaka Serve with: Green salad Dessert: Set Lemon Posset
FRIDAY	Gluten-free porridge with usual milk and Apricot Compôte	Banana	Mushroom Risotto Serve with: Cherry tomatoes Dessert: Classic Fruit Salad
SATURDAY	Banana and Blueberry Muffin	Chocolate Crispie Cake	Chicken, Lemon and Mint Risotto Serve with: Steamed curly kale Dessert: Instant Mango Sorbet
SUNDAY	Potato waffles and baked beans	Flapjacks	Sunday roast with rest of family Dessert: Apple and Blackberry Crumble

MID-AFTERNOON	TEA
ce cakes and gluten- ee breadsticks	Meatballs with Quinoa and gluten-free pasta Serve with: Tomato and Vegetable Sauce, Steamed broccoli Dessert: Tropical Fruit Salad
rapes	Chicken with Lemon, Garlic and Parlsey Serve with: Potato, Pea and Parsnip Cakes Dessert: Melon slices
ople Flapjack	Chicken in Coconut Milk Serve with: Plain boiled rice Dessert: Berry Fruit Salad
elon slices	Chicken Stir-fry Serve with: Plain boiled rice Dessert: Bananas and Cinnamon
emon Biscuit	Cottage Pie Serve with: Peas Dessert: Sliced apple and blackberries
arrot sticks and Red epper and Chickpea dip	Vegetable Chilli Serve with: Plain boiled rice Dessert: Orange
anana	Tomato and Vegetable Sauce with gluten-free pasta Dessert: Vanilla Coconut Panna Cotta

By now your toddler will be enjoying a huge variety of foods and enjoying social mealtimes with the rest of the family, hopefully with you all eating the same or very similar food. At this point you can feel really pleased with yourself that your baby is now fully weaned, and that you have done a fabulous job of introducing them to a lifetime of enjoying food and eating well.

NOTES

INDEX

ADDITIONAL INFORMATION

The first place to get advice about your child's allergy should always be your doctor and/or dietitian, but if you want to do a bit more research yourself there are lots of charities with very helpful websites. Websites change and new ones pop up, but at the time of writing these were all correct.

ALLERGY CHARITIES AND HELPFUL WEBSITES

WWW.ACTIONAGAINSTALLERGY.CO.UK

Provides a range of information about allergy.

WWW.ALLERGYUK.ORG

National charity established to represent people with allergy, food intolerance and chemical sensitivity.

WWW.ANAPHYLAXIS.ORG.UK

Provides guidance and information for people affected by life-threatening allergies.

WWW.ASTHMA.ORG.UK

While not a food allergy, we know that often children with food allergy suffer with other problems such as asthma.

WWW.BABYCENTRE.CO.UK

Online resource for new and expectant parents.

WWW.BLISS.ORG.UK

Charity supporting premature babies, with plenty of advice for weaning premature babies.

WWW.COELIAC.ORG.UK

A charity with invaluable resources for those with coeliac disease or gluten allergy.

WWW.ECZEMA.ORG

Plenty of information for eczema and dermatitis sufferers.

WWW.EFANET.ORG

Useful information about asthma and allergy.

WWW.FABED.CO.UK

Providing support for families affected by eosinophilic disorders.

WWW.LALECHE.ORG.UK

Breastfeeding support.

WWW.NCT.ORG.UK

The National Childbirth Trust is the UK's largest parenting charity.

WWW.NHS.UK

National Health Service website.

DIRECTORY OF READY-MADE FREE-FROM FOODS AND ESSENTIAL INGREDIENTS

Please have a look at our website www.foodallergymums.co.uk where we list all of our children's favourite ready-made, free-from foods. From bread, pasta and flour to biscuits, chocolate, and puddings to spreads, mayonnaise and sauces, we've compiled a comprehensive list of delicious free-from foods and basic ingredients that will help make life a little easier and supplement your home-cooked meals. It's surprising how many good products there are out there and ones that suit almost any combination of food allergies.

Follow us on twitter @foodallergymums and on Facebook [f] The Allergy-Free Family and Baby & Toddler Cookbooks

Also available from Orion

THE ALLERGY-FREE
FAMILY COOKBOOK